Thomas Lever

Sermons

1550

Thomas Lever

Sermons
1550

ISBN/EAN: 9783337112394

Printed in Europe, USA, Canada, Australia, Japan

Cover: Foto ©Lupo / pixelio.de

More available books at **www.hansebooks.com**

English Reprints.

THOMAS LEVER, M.A.

Fellow and Preacher of St. John's College, Cambridge.

SERMONS.
1550.

CAREFULLY EDITED BY
EDWARD ARBER,
Associate, King's College, London, F.R.G.S., &c.

LONDON:
5 QUEEN SQUARE, BLOOMSBURY, W.C.

nt. Stat. Hall.]   15 November, 1870.   [*All Rights reserved.*

English Reprints.

THOMAS LEVER, M.A.

Fellow and Preacher of St. John's College, Cambridge.

SERMONS.
1550.

CAREFULLY EDITED BY

EDWARD ARBER,

Affociate, King's College, London, F.R.G.S., &c.

LONDON:
5 QUEEN SQUARE, BLOOMSBURY, W.C.

Ent. Stat. Hall.]   15 November, 1870.   [*All Rights referved.*

CONTENTS.

NOTES of the Life and Writings of Thomas Lever,   8

INTRODUCTION, ... 9

BIBLIOGRAPHY, ... 17

I. *THE SERMON IN THE SHROUDS OF ST. PAUL'S CHURCH,* 19

    Septuagefima Sunday,
    'Hys fourth Sunday after twelfe tyde,' } 2 Feb. 1550.

TEXT. From the Epistle of the day. Rom. iii. 1-3.

II. *THE SERMON BEFORE KING EDWARD VI.,*   53

    Mid-Lent Sunday, 16 March 1550.

TEXT. From the Gospell of the day. John vi.

III. *THE SERMON AT PAUL'S CROSS,*   91

    Second Sunday in Advent, 14 December 1550.

   1. The Epistle [to the Counsell].
   2. The Sermon.
     No particular TEXT.

NOTES
of
The LIFE and WRITINGS
of
THOMAS LEVER, M.A.,

In succession, Fellow, Preacher and Master of St. John's College, Cambridge; Pastor in exile of the English Church at Aarau; Prebend of Durham Cathedral, Master of Sherburn Hospital for the poor.

The earliest account of our Author is the following brief contemporary one by John Bale:—
"Thomas Leuerus, patria Lancastriensis, insignis collegij, diuo Euangelistæ Ioanni apud Cantabrigiensis sacri, olim præses: nunc autem Anglorum ecclesiæ, quæ est in Arouia Heluetiorum urbe, primarius pastor; pius certè theologus, uitiorum osor, uirtutumque in omni mansuetudine seminator, in idiomate uulgari ad suos Anglos scripsit.

Semitam rectam ad Christum,   Lib. 1. *Cum uidissem meam in Anglia moram ac.*
In orationem Dominicam,   Lib. 1. *Propter laborem inopum et pauperum.*
Conciones aliquot
Atque alia.
Viuit Arouiæ, in uinea Domini fortiter laborans." *Script. Illust. Cent. ix.* 96, *p.* 762. *Ed.* 1557-9.

    1509. **Apr. 22. Henry VIII. begins to reign.**
 1542. Lever takes his B.A.
 1543. Is admitted Fellow of his college.
 1545. He takes his M.A. *Cooper, Ath. Cantab.* i. 366. *Ed.* 1858.
  St. Mary's vicarage, Burwell, was given by the King to the University of Cambridge, but only obtained by payment of £600 [= £9000 now] to Sir Edward, afterwards Lord North. This was the first occasion of emptying the University chest. It is denounced by Lever to King Edward VI. at *p.* 80.

    1547. **Jan. 28. Edward VI. ascends the throne.**
 1548. JULY 3. Lever is admitted a senior Fellow of St. John's College.
   SEPT. 22. He is appointed a College preacher: from which it is supposed that he was previously ordained.
   For public commotions in **1549–1550**: see *pp.* 15, 16.
 1550. FEB. 2. *Septuagesima Sunday.* Lever preaches the first of the three sermons here printed, in the Shrouds of St. Paul's church, London.
   MAR. 16. *Mid-Lent Sunday.* Lever preaches the second of these sermons before the King at Court.
   APR. 1. Bp. N. Ridley is translated from Rochester to London. Lever refers to him at *p.* 78.
   APR. "It was ordered that whosoever should have ecclesiastical benefices granted them by the King, should preach before him in or out of Lent, and that every Sunday there should be a sermon at Court."—*J. Strype, Eccles. Mem.* ii. 334. *Ed.* 1822.
   APR. 9. Lever's two sermons of this year are printed or reprinted, and finished on this day.
   JUNE 24. Bp. Ridley ordains 25 deacons before the high altar of St. Paul's, including Lever and John Fox the martyrologist. —*Strype, idem.* ii. 402.
   AUG. 10. Bp. Ridley ordains at Fulham several persons deacons: and his chaplain, John Bradford, with Thomas Lever, priests. —*Strype, idem.* ii. 403.

Dec. 12. *Second Sunday in Advent.* Lever preaches the Third of these sermons at Paul's Cross.

Dec. . This sermon he immediately publishes with a preface.

1551. April. Sedburgh (Yorkshire) Grammar School refounded by a grant of the King in part the result of Lever's previous exposure of its spoliation: see *p.* 81.

1551. Lowndes quotes the following work by Lever:—
"A Meditation vpon the Lordes Prayer, made at Sayncte Mary Wolchurche, London. Anno MDLi. Lond. by Iohn Daye. 16mo."

1551. Dec. 10–**1553**, Sept. 28. Thomas Lever, Seventh Master of St. John's College, Cambridge.

1552. He takes his B.D.

1552. July 7. Roger Ascham writing to Sir W. Cecil from Villacho in Carinthia: thus refers to the then Master of John's.

"Mr *Leaver* wrote vnto me a ioyfull lettre of Mr. *Cheekes* most happie recouery, praying to god in his lettre that *England* may be thankfull to god, for restoring soch a man agein to the King, and well prayed trewlie; but I am thus firmelie perswaded, that god wist and wold we wold be thankfull and therfore bestowed this benefit vpon vs. Gods wroth, I trust, is satisfied in punishing diuers orders of the realme for their misorder, with taking away singular men from them, as Learnyng by Mr. *Bucer*, Counsell by Mr. *Denny*, nobilitie by the two yong *Dukes*, Courting by ientle *Blage*, S. *Iohns* by good *Eland*. But if Lerning, Counsell, Nobilitie, Courte, *Cambridge* shold haue bene all punisshed at ones, by taking away mr. *Cheke*, then I wold haue thought our mischeef had bene so mochs as did crye to god for a generall plage, in taking away soch a general and onely man as mr. Cheeke is.—*Lansdowne MSS.* 3, *fol.* 1.

[**1553.**—Notwithstanding the pressures this and other colleges were under in point of maintenance, which Mr. Leaver complains of in his sermons, occasioned by the courtiers' invading church preferments (that were intended as rewards of learning) by racking their tenants, formerly accustomed to easy rents whilst a great part of the lands of the nation were in the hands of the church, by their neglect of hospitality which ought to have been kept up, and by their want of charity which had formerly been maintained, yet the college flourished in learning, and what usually attends it, in the true religion. The reformation nowhere gained more ground or was more zealously maintained, than it did here under this master's example and the influence of his government, as appeared best in the day of trial, when he with twenty-four of his fellows, quitted their preferments to preserve their innocence.—T. *Baker, B.D., Hist. of St. John's Coll. i.* 132. *Ed. by J. E. Mayor,* 1869.]

1553. July 6. 𝔐ary succeeds to the crown.

Lever and twenty-four Fellows resign and leave the country. Roger Ascham thus refers to this exodus in his *Scholemaster*:—

"Yea *S. Iohnes* did then so florish, as Trinitie college, that Princelie house now, at the first erection, was but *Colonia deducta* out of *S. Iohnes*, not onelie for their Master, fellowes, and scholers, but also, which is more, for their whole, both order of learning, and discipline of maners. . . . . *S. Iohnes* stoode in this state, vntill those heuie tymes, and that greuous change that chanced. An. 1553. whan mo perfite scholers were dispersed from thence in one moneth, than many yeares can reare vp againe." *p.* 135. *Ed.* 1870.

1554. July. John Knox in a 'Comparyson betwixte England and Iuda before their destruction' in his *Godly letter sent too the fayethfull in London / Newcastle / Barwyke / &c.,* thus writes

'That godly and feruent man mayster Lever / playnlye spake the desolacion off thys common wealthe.'

1554. Bp. Ridley in his *Piteous Lamentation on the state of the Church of England*, writes:—"As for Latimer, Leuer, Bradford, and Knox, their tongues were so sharp, they ripped in so deep in their galled backs, to haue purged them no doubt of that filthy matter that was festered in their hearts, of insatiable couetousness, of filthy carnality and voluptuousness, of intolerable ambition and pride, of ungodly loathsomeness to hear poor men's causes, and to hear God's word, that these men of all other these magistrates then could neuer abide."

1554. OCT. 25. Lever writes from Zurich to Bradford:—"I have seen the places, noted the doctrine and discipline, and talked with the learned men of Argentine, Basil, Zurich, Bern, Lausan, and Geneva; and I have had experience in all these places of sincere doctrine, godly order and doctrine and great learning, and especially of such virtuous learning, diligence, and charity, in Bullinger at Zurich, and in Calvin at Geneva, as doth much advance God's glory, unto the edifying of Christ's church, with the same religion for the which you be now in prison."—*Writings of Bradford*, ii. 137. Ed. 1853.

1555. FEB. 11. Bradford in his *Farewell to Cambridge*, dated "Out of prison, ready to the stake, the 11th of February, *anno* 1555;" writes:—

"Call to mind the threatenings of God now something seen by thy children, Lever and others. Let the exile of Lever, Pilkington, Grindal, Haddon, Horne, Scory, Ponet, &c., something awake thee. Let the imprisonment of thy dear sons, Cranmer, Ridley, and Latimer, move thee. Consider the martyrdom of thy chickens, Rogers, Saunders, Taylor: and now cast not away the poor admonition of me going to be burned also, and to receive the like crown of glory of my fellows."—*Writings*, i. 445. Ed. 1848.

1556. Lever in a preface dated 'at Geneva, 1556,' prints many copies of a treatise *Of the right way from Danger of Sinne, &c.* See **1571.**

1558 Nob. 17. Elizabeth begins to reign.

1559. APR. Lever marries a widow, who has three children already.
1560. JULY 10. He speaks of the birth of a daughter.

Lever returns to England, soon after the Queen's accession, with more Puritan views than ever.

Sherburn Hospital was founded by Hugh de Pudsey [who became Bp. of Durham on 20 Dec. 1153, acquired by purchase Earl of Northumberland in 1190; *d.* 3 Mar. 1195; æt. 70,] about 1181, in the time of the great plague of leprosy in England in the reign of Henry II., for the reception of sixty-five poor lepers, with a master and other officers to superintend the same. Great abuses being complained of, Thomas Langley, another Bp. of Durham [bet. 17 May 1406—28 Nov. 1437] issued fresh ordinances on 22 July 1434, which *inter alia* directed that the future master should be in clerical orders.

It appears that the leprosy (for the relief of those under which affliction this hospital was founded) was at that time almost eradicated, for Bp. Langley directs, that in the remembrance of the original foundation, two lepers should be received into the hospital, if they could be found, but to be kept apart from the rest of the people admitted to the house. To those, thirteen poor people were to be added, to be provided with meat and drink of tenpence value every week, or tenpence of ready money at their own option, and have yearly the sum of 6s. 8d. for fuel and cloaths, and to mess and lodge in the same house, and daily to attend mass. Upon the death of a brother, another poor man to be chosen by the master within fifteen days, under the penalty of paying a mark to the fabric of the church at Durham. An old woman of good character was to be provided at the master's expense, to attend the brethren, wash their linen, and do other offices. The master to have the care of all the goods and buildings of the hospital, and to take an oath for the due performance of all things stipulated by those ordinances.—J. Hutchison's *Hist. of Durham*, ii. pp. 589, 607. *Ed.* 1780.

1562. JAN. 28. Thomas Lever was born in Lancashire, collated to Sherburn hospital. *Idem. p.* 594.

1563. FEB. 2. Lever is made a Prebend of Durham Cathedral.

1567. Lever supplies *A preface, shewing the true understanding of God's word, and the right use of God's works and benefits, evident and easy to be seen in the exercise of these Meditations*: and also *A meditation on the Tenth Commandment* to the edition of this year, of *Godly Meditations, &c. &c.*, made by John Bradford. [Reprinted in Townsend's *Writings of Bradford. Ed.* 1848.]

1567. He is deprived of his Prebendship.

1568. FEB. 24. There is a characteristic letter of Lever's showing that he was the same zealous and disinterested Reformer and Protestant to the latter end of his life, as when he preached these Sermons.

Grace and peace in *Christ*. For that god hath placed you in authoritie and fauer with the Quenes Maiestie, so as heretofore I and mani others haue bi your meanes had quietnes, libertie and comfort to preach the gospell of *Christ*: therefore of Christian charitie, and bonden dutie must we daili prai, and vse all godli indeuor for the continuance of the same.

And so now as more willing then able to render due thankfulnes vnto god, the Quenes Maiestie and vnto your honors, I haue here noted summe such things as make mich to the subuersion, or preseruation of godlie honor.

Gen. 34. The *Sichemites* receiuing circumcision partli for voluptuousnes, and partli for couiteousnes were all vtterli destroied, w[h]ich is a terrible threatning to *Englande*: where as mani euen so farre receiue and refuse religion, as semeth to be for pleasure or gaine worldli.   And *Iosu.* 7. The armie of the *Israellites* polluted with the couiteous spoile of *Achan* cold neither vse sufficient power, nor a good policie against their and gods ennimies, vntill that offence was confessed, and such corruption vterli abolished from amorge gods people: and then did god giue vnto his people the vse of power and policie, to preuaile against their ennimies. So *England* being polluted with mich couiteous spoile especialli of impropriations, grammer scoles and other prouision for the pore, can not vse power and policie to preuaile against the ennimies of god and godli religion, if it sinke still into such corruption, as causeth more sclander, and danger daili to incresse vnto the cheife professers, and promoters of good religion.

And certenli the necessari reuenues of the prince, the bishops, other estates, and the vniuersities, do as yet rather sinke into the corruption then stand vpon the profets, of improperations.

Wherefore in the vniuersities, and els where no standing but sinking doth appere; when as the office and liuing of a minister shalbe taken from him, that once lawfulli admitted hath euer since diligentli preached, because he now refuseth prescription of man in apparrell: and the name, liuing and office of a minister of gods worde, allowed vnto him that neither can nor will preach, except it be *pro forma tantum*, to kepe gods commandments summe times *per alium*, euer obseruing the prescription of man in wairing apparell and reding *per se*.

Also *Ezech.* 14. When as bi plaines of the prophets notable idolatrie was reproued in *Israell*, and at the same time the Elders of *Israell* keping their idols in their hartes, and setting their stombling blockes afore their faces, wold yet bi hearing the prophet and worde of god, seme to be godli: then such Elders and prophettes hearing and answaring, according to the vncleines of their owne hartes, were both iustli deceiued and destroied of god. Like wise now is notable papistrie in *England* and *Scotland* proued and proclaimed bi preaching of the gospell, to be idolatrie and treason, and how such idolatrie and treason is yet norrished in the hartes of mani god knoweth, and how the old stombling stockes be sett openli of mani things in mani places, and especialli of the crucifix in *England*, and of the masse in *Scotland* afore the faces of the hieghest, is daili to be seen of idolators and traitors with reioiecing and hoping of a dai; and of christian faithfull obedient subiects with sorrow of harte and feare of the state.

And if in the ministre and ministers of gods worde, the sharpnes of salt bi doctrine, to mortifie affections, be reiected, and ceremonial seruice with flateri, to fede affections, reteined; then doth *Christ* threaten such treding vnder fote, as no power or policie can withstand or abide. Further more vnder *Ahasuerus*, the moost faithfull people of god and obedient subiectes were then falseli accused to be breakers of the kings lawes, and so brought into extreme danger and destresse. Then *Ester* the quene aduertised bi *Mardochæ* what occasion god had offered vnto her to help his people, did take and vse the same occasion, vnto the moost comfortable deliverance of them, and the greattest incresse and stai of her honor and state.

Contrariwise *Ezech*. 29. *Egipt* as a staf of rede failing breaking and hurting gods people, in their destresse leaning and trusting vnto it, did bi the iust iudgment of god loose honor and power, man and beast, and so was with dishonor brought to desolation.

The most godli and faithfull subiects be maini times worst suspected and reported, and so brought into greatest destresse and danger, that bi gods prouidence wonderfulli to gods glorie thei mai be preserued and prosper, seing their ennimies aud conterfeited frendes tried, and destroied by gods iust iudgements.

Now therefore mi praier vnto god, and writing to your honors is, that authoritie in *England*, and especialli you mai for sincere religion refuse pleasure and gaine worldli, and not for worldli praise, profet or pleasure receiue, refuse or abuse religion corruptli: not to allowe ani such corruption amonge *protestants*, being gods seruants, as shold make *papistes* to ioie and hope for a dai, being gods ennimies: but rather cause such abolishing of inward *papistrie*, and outward monuments of the same as shold cause idolatrous traitors to greue, and faithfull subiects to be glad: such casting forth of the vnsaueri ministre and ministers of gods worde as might make onli such as haue the sauerines of doctrine and edification to be allowed in that office, seing such ministre onli mai preserue princes, and prestes and people from casting and treading vnder fote: and so not deceiuing and leaning the godli in destresse, to perisshe with the vngodli through vngodlines, but euer traueling to deliuer, defend, and help the godli, be bi gods prouidence and promise deliuered and preserued from all danger, into continuance and incresse of godli honor: which god for his mercies in *Christ* grant, vnto the Quenes Magestie, vnto you, and all other of her honorable counsell. Amen. Scriblet at *Sherborn* house by *Duresme* the 24 of februarij.

Bi yours at comandment faithfull in *Christ*

Thomas Leuer.

Addressed on } To the right honorable Lord Robert Erle of Leicestre and Sr
the back } William Cicell Knight and to either of them, at the Court.

Endorsed 24 Febr. 1568 Mr. Levor to my L. of Leices. and myself. Adviseth yat ye refusing or receiuing of religion may not depend vpon Worldly respects. *Lands. MS*. 11, *Art*. 5.

1569. Nov. 14—**1570.** Jan. The rebellion in the North. It began at Durham. It must have been a dangerous time for such an ultra protestant as Lever.

1571. Lever issues a second edition of *A treatise of the right way from Danger of Sinne* **and vengeance in this** *wicked worlde*, *vnto godly wealth* **and** *saluation in Christe*: in the Epistle, dated at London 1571, to which, he states:—

"Of this matter did I wryte a little Booke beyng in Geneua in the time of Queene Maries raigne, when I was there by diuerse English men mooued and requested too cause it too bee printed; and so then with a lyttle Preface I dyd send many of those Bookes so printed, intoo this Realme of Englande.

And nowe finding none of those Bookes too be solde in anie place, but being of some desired too peruse one of them (which was founde in a freendes hande) and putte it too printing agayn, with some admonition meete for this tyme, I haue written this Epistle or Preface. . . ."

1572. The revised and corrected edition of these Sermons is published.

1572. T. Baker, B D., in a folio commonplace book, now *Harl. MS.* 7048, has copied 'a long scroll, on several sheets, pasted together' and printed by Henrie Bynneman, for Humfrey Toy, 1572, but apparently never published: of what is virtually the Cambridge Calendar for that year. The number of Scholars of all the degrees in the Universitie was then 1684. From this we quote the *Daily exercises for Schollers* by way of comparison to Lever's account in 1550, at *pp.* 121, 122.

Euery worke daye throughout the whole yeare, in euery Colledge are celebrated Morning Prayers from fiue of the Clock untill sixe / at what time also some Common Place is expounded by one of ye Fellows in order after that he hath bene Master of Arte. That done from seuen of the Clocke untill eight in all Colledges are plainly and distinctly taught and reade Logicke and Philosophie Lectures. From eight of the Clock vntill Eleuen, ordinarie Lectures and publicke Disputations are exercised / and reade in the Common Schooles. *p.* 541.

1575. A third edition of *The right way*, &c., was issued: printed by H. Bynneman.

At the end of it is (apparently reprinted) *A meditation vppon the Lordes prayer.* A copy is in the British Museum.

1577. JULY. On a journey home to the hospital of Sherburn, (which he was permitted to retain on account of the scarcity of preachers, though deprived of his prebend for non-conformity) falling sick by the way, died at Ware the beginning of July 1577, his body was brought to and interred adjoining the south wall within the altar rails of the chapel of Sherburn hospital, under a blue marble stone, whereon is cut a cross flory with a bible and chalice, . . . and on a brass plate

THOMAS LEAVER PREACHER
TO KING EDWARD THE SIXTE.
HE DIED IN IVLY 1577.

His brother Ralph succeeded him as Master, being collated on 16 July 1577.—*Hutchinson, Hist. of Durham,* ii. 589.

Thomas Baker calls Lever 'one of the best masters as well as one of the best men the college [of St. John's, Cambridge] ever bred.'

In Haynes' Burghley Papers p 362 there is a letter from L. to Sir F Knollys & Sir W Cecil from Coventry 17 Sept regarding the conduct of the Lodge by Lord Robert Dudley." Retro Rev 2 Series Vol I 1827 p 229

INTRODUCTION.

Notwithstanding all that has been faid and written; the Story of the Englifh Reformation has by no means been fully and exactly recovered. It was the ftrangeft and greateft Change that had occurred in England, fince fhe had abandoned Paganifm. There happened alfo to come at the fame time, a moft trying Social Progrefs; which was quite diftinct from it, which was greatly mifunderftood at the time, and which has fince been fometimes confounded with it.

The Reformation was fome twenty-five years old, when thefe Sermons were uttered. Inftrumentally, it had been the work of many Scholars, of fome of the Town Clergy, Monks, &c., of Merchants and the like, and of the Lollards among the lower claffes. It began before Henry courted Anne Boleyn, and would have certainly come to pafs had he or fhe died in Wolfey's life time: but the Divorce Queftion became for ever mixed up with the change of Faith and Worfhip among the people of England.

The Reformation—as in the cafe of the firft foundation of Chriftianity, as indeed of neceffity muft be the cafe of the eftablifhment of any religion upon earth—began with a few. Thefe fearchers after Truth and Holinefs went on leavening the people. The Reformers and the Reformed had been and were even now far outnumbered by the Inland Catholic population: the country Clergy, Gentry, Farmers, and Labourers. It was a long conflict between the Government and the more active Intelligence of the Minority in the Nation, refiding in Univerfity and fouthern cities: and the Confervatifm of a Majority living in purely agricultural diftricts and in the remoter northern towns.

The procefs of the Reformation was moft difficult to the unlettered people. All that was concrete in a gorgeous ceremonial and worfhip was replaced by the fimple enunciation of principles of life and conduct, and their application to all conditions of fociety. The Mafs and the Proceffion were fucceeded by the long Sermon, which even now fends fome of its hearers into a quiet fleep, and which lafted three or four hours, as Latimer intended his Sermon in this fame Lent to have done. What had, for ages paft, been confidered as unerring authority in all matters towards God, had now been indignantly abandoned as a prepofterous fraud. Roods, fhrines, and other vehicles of adoring worfhip alfo became a mock and bye-word. To crown all; in place of the comfort and certainty of a pretentioufly infallible fyftem could only be offered inducements to inceffant ftriving after that which is True, Right, and Pure. The Reformation in leading the people to a higher life, impofed upon them the arduous toil of the afcent.

What then was the tafk of the Reformers: firft in unlearning and in learning themfelves; then in teaching, under all conceivable oppofition, the people. The firſt Reformers engaged againſt enormous odds. They faced a Hierarchy that could, by power of Law, fmite down its antagoniſts even unto death. So that moſt of the Reformers came to be judicially murdered for their opinions: and then, by a ſtrange change of fate, fome of their Judges followed them in fuffering like cruel injuſtice.

Such furvivors of this firſt Band, as efcaped the block and the ſtake, re-appeared in public life, like Latimer and Coverdale, foon after the acceffion of Edward VI.: and then regained more than their priſtine influence with the Reformed.

With thefe, joined a fecond race of Reformers, their fpiritual children, fuch as Lever, Bradford, Knox, and others. The Lent of 1550, witneffed Latimer preaching his laſt Sermon at Court, his *Ultimum Vale* to Edward VI., and Lever's firſt addrefs to the King and Nation. One generation was therein overlapping the fecond.

II. The Reformation found England fettling down from the long anarchy of the Wars of the Rofes. From the beginning of the century there had been a general Rife in Prices: fometimes a factitious and paffing one, by Speculators (Foreſtallers or Regrators as they were then called) rigging the market; but alfo through the increafing wealth of the country. This had nothing effentially to do with the Reformation. It was not the cafe in Germany and Switzerland at the time. It was the recovery of this country from the Civil Wars.

But this enrichment was not general. The rich became richer, and the poor more deſtitute. There were few to take the part of the poor, but the Preachers. As we liſten to Lever we are often reminded of our prefent Newfpapers. The Pulpit then did the work of our Platform, and the Prefs as well. So thefe Sermons, dealing with troubles and abufes all round, are a perfect revelation to us of thofe times. The current events, and what is ſtill more valuable, the general talk and impreffion of the Court and the City in 1550; photographed in them, conſtitute them moſt valuable records of the domeſtic hiſtory of England in that year; while the fuperlative moral bravery of the preacher that could fpeak fuch home truths fo plainly to the King, the Counfell, and that quick and high-fpirited People, cannot but win our admiration of the man.

It is impoffible here even to touch upon every fraud attacked by the Preacher: but two chief points may be confidered, by way of preparation to the Sermons themfelves.

INCLOSURES.—Wool was and had long been the ſtaple product of England. The rife in the Price of Wool was depopulating the country, defpite all ordinances and ſtatutes whatfoever. Sir T. Moore, in his Latin *Utopia*, thus proteſts, in the perfon of Raphael Hythlodaye, againſt the rapacity of landlords of all ſorts anterior to 1516.

> But yet this is not only the necessary cause of stealing. There is an other, whych, as I suppose, is p[ro]per and peculiar to you Englishmen alone. What is that, quod the Cardinal? forsoth my lorde (quod I) your shepe that were wont to be so meke and tame, and so smal eaters, now, as I heare saye, be become so great denowerers and so wylde, that they eate vp, and swallow downe the very men them selfes. They consume, destroye, and denoure whole fieldes, howses, and cities. For looke in what partes of the realme doth growe the fynest, and therfore dearest woll, there noble men, and gentlemen: yea and certeyn Abbottes, holy men no doubt, not contenting them selfes with the yearly reuenues and profytes, that were wont to grow to theyr forefathers and predecessours of their landes, nor beynge content that they liue in rest and pleasure nothinge profiting, yea much noyinge the weale publique: leaue no grounde for tillage, thei inclose al into pastures: thei throw doune houses: they plucke downe townes, and leaue nothing standynge, but only the churche to be made a shepehowse. And as thoughe you loste no small quantity of grounde by forestes, chases, laundes, and parkes, those good holy men turne all dwellinge places and all that glebeland into desolation and wildernes. Therfore that on couetous and vnsatiable cormaraunte and very plage of his natyue contrey maye compasse aboute and inclose many thousand akers of grounde to gether within one pale or hedge, the husbandmen be thrust owte of their owne, or els either by coueyne and fraude, or by violent oppression they be put besydes it, or by wronges and iniuries thei be so weried, that they be compelled to sell all: by one meanes therfore or by other, either by hooke or crooke they muste needes departe awaye, poore, selye, wretched soules, men, women, husbands, wiues, fatherlesse children, widowes, wofull mothers, with their yonge babes, and their whole houshold smal in substance, and muche in numbre, as husbandrye requireth manye handes. Awaye thei trudge, I say, out of their knowen and accustomed houses, fyndynge no place to reste in. All their housholdestuffe, whiche is verye little woorthe, thoughe it myght well abide the sale: yet beeynge sodainely thruste oute, they be con-trayned to sell it for a thing of nought. And when they haue wandered abrode tyll that be spent, what can they then els doo but steale, and then iustly pardy be hanged, or els go about a beggyng. And yet then also they be caste in prison as vagaboundes, because they go aboute and worke not: whom no man wyl set a worke, though thei neuer so willyngly profre themselues therto. For one Shephearde or Heardman is ynoughe to eate vp that grounde with cattel, to the occupiyng wherof aboute husbandrye manye handes were requisite. And this is also the cause why victualles be now in many places dearer. Yea, besides this the price of wolle is so rysen, that poore folkes, which were wont to worke it, and make cloth therof, be nowe hable to bye none at all. And by thys meanes verye manye be forced to forsake worke, and to geue them selues to idlenesse. For after that so much grounde was inclosed for pasture, an infinite multitude of shepe dyed of the rotte, suche vengeaunce God toke of their inordinate and vnsaciable couetousnes, sendinge amonge the shepe that pestiferous morrein, whiche much more iustely shoulde haue fallen on the shepemasters owne heades. And though the number of shepe increase neuer so faste, yet the price falleth not one myte, because there be so fewe sellers. For they be almooste all comen into a fewe riche mennes handes, whome no neade forceth to sell before they lust, and they luste not before they maye sell as deare as they luste." *pp.* 40-42. *Ed.* 1869.

Ever ſince Moore wrote, the ſtate of things of which he thus complains had continued to increaſe rather than diminiſh.

The Rev. F. W. Ruſſell in his *Kett's Rebellion in Norfolk*, Ed. 1859, 4to, tells us that "at this time, the arable land of any village or townſhip, known as 'the field'—a name ſtill in common uſe—was ſubdivided by ridges called 'bawlkes' into 'lands' belonging to the different proprietors, who cultivated them and took the produce; but when 'the corne was inned and harueſt don,' then all had right of common over the whole. Juſt prior to Kett's rebellion, the practice began to be generally adopted by thoſe who had two or more lying together, to encloſe theſe 'lands' as well as others, viz., the waſte lands of the manor, that ought to be common, and it was againſt ſuch encloſures that the efforts of Kett and his aſſociates were eſpecially directed."

A Commiſſion to redreſs Encloſures was iſſued by King Edward's Counſell on 2 June 1548. In a ſpeech of one of the Commiſſioners, Mr. John Hales, preſerved by Strype, we have the following official definition : —

But first, to declare unto you what is meant by this word *incloſures*. It is not taken where a man doth enclose and hedge in his own proper ground, where no man hath commons. For such incloſure where no man hath commons. For such incloſure is very beneficial to the commonwealth; it is a cause of great increase of wood, but it is meant therby, when any man hath taken away and enclosed any other mens commons, or hath pulled down houses of husbandry, and converted the lands from tillage to pasture. This is the meaning of the word, and we pray you to remember it.

To defeat these statuts, as we be informed, some have not pulled down their houses, but maintain them; howbeit no person dwelleth therin ; or if there be, it is but a shepheard or a milkmaid, and convert the lands from tillage to pasture : and some about one hundred acres of ground, or more or less, make a furrow, and sow that ; and the rest they till not, but pasture their sheep. And some take the lands from their houses, and occupy them in husbandry ; but let the houses out to beggars and old poor people. Some, to colour the multitude of their sheep, father them on their children, kinsfolks, and servants. All which be but only crafts and subtilties to defraud the laws, such as no good man will use, but rather abhor.—*Eccles. Mem.* II. ii. 361. Ed. 1822.

Such was one form of the ſtruggle for the poſſeſſion of the land of the country, on account of its increaſing value. Another form of this covetouſneſs (and can we wonder at Latimer and Lever denouncing covetouſneſs ſo much !) conſiſted in

IMPROPRIATIONS OF ECCLESIASTICAL BENEFICES; which were the poſſeſſion of their revenues by corporations, non-reſident clergy, or laymen ; and the delegation of the ſpiritual duties of the benefice to a Curate : and of the temporal duties (collecting the tithes, keeping up hoſpitality, and the like) unto a Farmer. This abuſe alſo exiſted long before the Reformation.

Sir Francis Bygod [? of Mogreve Caſtle in Blakemore], who on a ſudden joined, and by joining, ruined *The Pilgrimage of Grace*, in January 1537 : for which he was hanged at Tyburn in the June following. Froude [*Hiſt. of England, iii.* 193. Ed. 1858] wrote a ſtrange tract entitled *A Treatiſe concernynge impropriations of beneficies*, printed by T. Godfrey, without date: but certainly after the birth of the Princeſs Elizabeth (7 Sept. 1533) and before the ſuppreſſion of the leſſer Monaſteries (with leſs than £200 [=£3000 now] a year) in March 1536; ſay therefore about 1534.

In this farrago of creeds, Bygod calls Henry the 'ſupreme

hed,' the Pope the 'gret draffacke of Rome,' approves 'of the preaching of the Gofpel,' and yet talks of the 'bleſſed Maſs.' Notwithſtanding all this, Bygod—apparently then a 'Six Articles' man—could write to good purpoſe on his grievance.

But me thynketh I here you whysper that ye be no murtherers / theues / pykers / sacrylegans / nor yet none of all this geare / No ar nat? Well / than I se well we must haue more to do with you. For as moche as ye denye the cryme layde vnto your charge. You shall vnderstande that good and vertuouse men before our dayes / whiche loued the wyll of god / whiche loued his holy pleasure / whiche regarded his commaundement / whose medytatyons and studye both day and nighte was / to set forth his glorie / to auaunce his blessed worde / and to maynteine the ministers of the same / dyd (no dout of it) with the consent of higher powers of kynges and of princes / and of their most honourable counsels / folowynge (in this behalfe) the olde lawe / for the most easyest waye and spedyest prouisyon / appoynt / assygne and ordeyne (for the same ministers to be maynteyned) decymations or tythes / wyllynge and myndynge by this good prouisyon / that within euery congregation or paryshe / the minister of goddes worde there / shulde be sure at all tymes of a lyuynge raysed and gathered of these sayde decymations / and therein to haue added a certayne name / callynge it a benefyce / personage or vycarage / and lyke wyse turnynge the name of a minister or curate / to the name of a persone or vycare. Furthermore orderynge that one man shall haue authoritie / as patrone / to name this parsone / and so to giue this same benefyce: albe[i]t / peraduenture that other in the same paryshe gyue as moche to the annuall lyuynge of the parsone as the patrone doth. Besydes this / they ordeyned him a mantion to dwel in among them / to th[e]entente that for his dilygente administration / he shulde haue euery thinge necessarye for him within his owne gouernance: yea / and haue it brought euen home vnto him / to dyspose at his pleasure / as it shall be most expedyent and necessary for him / that the more quyetly he mighte studye and apply him selfe to minister vnto them the pure worde of god / and to be euer redy at hande to enstructe them of all thinges necessarye for ye helth of their soules / and to be their trewe watchman and shepherde to take them from the rauysshynge wolfe / and lyke a good trew herdesman / a pastoure to go afore them in spirytuall and vertuouse conuersation: and euer whan they be scabbed to anoynte them gentely with the softe and swete salue of goddes worde / all rancoure and stryfe layde a parte. Nowe my maisters impropriated or improper maisters howe saye ye by youre fathers / haue nat you with your crafty collusyon / almooste throughe Englande / dystroyed these holy and godly prouysons / made for the mayntenance of goddes holy word / and for th[e]administratyon of this most blessed sacramentes / for the helth / welth / and saluatyon of mans soule / for the vpholdynge of the trewe and catholyque fayth / for the supportacyon of vertue / and dystruction of vyce. Have nat you (I saye) by the glykynge and gleynyng / snatchynge and scratchinge / tatchynge and patchynge / scrapinge and rakynge togyther of almost all the fatte benefyces within this realme and impropriatynge them vnto youre selues / distroyed this most godlye and holy prouision / bereyued the peple of ye worde of god / of ye trew knowlege of ye blessed sacramentes / of their trew beleue and faith in god the father / and the blode of Iesu Christ. For howe can the people haue any faith in god withoute preachinge? Howe shulde they haue any preachynge whan ye haue robbed them of their ministers? How shulde the ministers serue them whan ye haue robbed them of theire lyuynge? If the peple haue no faith how can they haue charyte? If they haue no charytie / what merueyle is it / if they ronne hedlonge and be caryed from one vyce to another / from one mischefe to another? Be nat ye th[e] occasion of all this? Who is elles I praye you? Haue nat ye the impropriations? Be the impropriacyons any thinge els sauynge benefyces as parsonages / and such lyke? Do we not say such an abbot is parsone here / suche a priour is parsone here? yea / suche a prioresse is parsone here?

After dealing with the objection 'We haue teachinge inough / and that there is neuer the lesse preachynge for you;' Bygod thus goes on.

But nowe ye wyll obiecte that no ordynaunce of god is broken / hindered / or prohibyted on your behalfe in this mater. For thoughe the benefyce be impropriate to a monster / I wolde saye to a monasterye / yet th[e]abbot or prioure appoynteth a monke or chanon to be the minister / and to preche the worde of god to the parysshe / who shall tarye and abyde amonge his parysshoners / and haue oute of the same benefyce a suffycyente lyuynge / and the reste thereof to come home to th[e]abbot and his bretherne: and this is no breakynge of goddes ordynaunce / but rather a turnynge of it to a better vse. Wherevnto I answere / that where any such vicare or minyster is instytuted of his abbot or priour / and trewly laboureth in th[e]administration of goddes worde / it is nat onely well done to gyue him a suffycyent lyuynge out of the same benefyce / but also he were wel worthy to haue it euerywhitte / and as for the rest that haboundeth / let him kepe hospytalyte / as Paule commaundeth / or of necessytie wylleth him to do / and I saye / there shall but lytell remayne to sende home to th[e]abbot / and if he do nat kepe hospytilyte of the rest / then is he a thefe and th[e]abbot another / for the rest is the poore indygentes. But howe faythfull and dilygent suche men be so instytuted by abbotes and priours to preache the worde of god / and howe sore they be therwith charged by their heedes. I thynke though I wolde cloke it / yet th[e]effecte wyl nat suffre it. Yet / I beleue rather that they ben the stronge persecutors of goddes worde / rather than the furtherers therof. . . .

But nowe these men beynge neuer without excuses / may peraduenture thinke this to be a good answere for me. We praye for the soules of them that haue improperated such benefyces vnto vs / and synge masse and diryge for them / and set vp tapers for them to burne both daye and night. Wherevnto fyrst I say / that if a man demaunded of you an accompte to be gyuen of youre so doynge / askynge you who taught you to apply ye blessed masse that waye / with the psalmes and lessons in the diryge conteyned / and desyred you to shew scripture for it. I thynke peraduenture that ye might come short home of a wyse answere / which if ye can make / I thinke ther is no man but he wyl be wel content ther with. . . .

Some men that fauoure these newe founde sectes / wyll peraduenture say: Well / yet it is better these monkes / chanons / and suche lyke haue the impropriatyons (whiche though they preche nat / yet they kepe some hospitalyte) rather than the seculer priestes shulde haue them / as they haue had before / which kepe no hospitalytie nor preche nother. To this it is easy to answere: That it is not mete that any man what soeuer he be / shuld receyue the benefyte or frute of a precher / onles he do his duty therfore. . . . .

Is it nat great pitye to se a man to haue thre or foure benefyces: yea peraduenture halfe a score or a dosyn / which he neuer cometh at / but setteth in euery one of them a syr[1] Iohn lacke laten / that can scarce rede his porteus / orels suche a rauenynge wolfe as canne do nothynge but denoure the sely shepe with his false doctryne / and sucke their substaunce from them. Lorde / if it be thy pleasure / ones haue mercye vpon vs / and gyue grace that we may haue some remedye founde for thys myschiefe / bothe of impropriatyons / and also of them that minister not the worde of god faythfully vpon their benefyces: as they ought to do: for I haue knowen suche / that whan they hauen rydden by a benefyce wherof they haue ben persone / they coulde natte tell that it was their benefyce. This is a wonderfull blyndnesse.

We have not space here to illustrate the great *fiasco* of the Suppression of the Monasteries, the decay of the Universities, the uprising of the lower classes against the Nobility and Gentry, the utter destitution of the poor, the pluralities of benefices, the general covetousness, and the other crying abuses denounced in these Sermons. Most of the complaints of that time have been ably collected by Mr. F. J. Furnivall, in his *Ballads from MSS.* Vol. I. Ed. 1868, to which we must refer our readers.

[1] The customary title of respect at this time for priests, as Esquire is now for the laity.

Introduction. 15

The beft fetting we can put to thefe difcourfes are the following brief extracts from Stowe, of the commotions of the two years 1549 and 1550—

1549. MAY. By meanes of a proclamation for inclosures, the commons of Somersetshire and Lincolnshire made a commotion, and brake vp certain parks of Sir *W. Herberts*, and Lord *Sturtons*, but sir *W. Herbert* slewe and executed many of those rebels.

JULY. The commons of Essex and Kent, Suffolk and Norfolk, rose against inclosures, and pulled down diuers parks and houses.

Also the commons of Cornewall and Deuonshire rose against the nobles and gentlemen, and required not onely that the inclosures might bee disparked, but also to haue their old religion, and act of sixe articles restored: these besieged the citie of Excester, which was valiantlie defended. Against these rebels was sent *John* L[ord]. *Russell* Lord priuy seale, with a number of souldiers, who entered the city of Excester the 5 of AUGUST, where they slew and took prisoners of the rebels more than 4000. and after hanged diuers of them in the towne and country about. The L[ord]. *Gray* was also sent with a number of strangers, Almaine and Germaine horsemen, who in diuers conflicts slewe manie people, and spoiled the country.

31 JULY. *William*, L[ord]. marques of Northampton, entred the city of Norwich, and on the next morning, the rebels also entred the towne, burned parte thereof, put the L[ord] marques to flight, and slew the L[ord] *Sheffield*.

22 JULY. In this meane time diuers persons were apprehended as aiders of of the foresaid rebels or reporters of their doinges, of the which one was the Bailife of Romford in Essex, hanged within Aldgate, and an other of Kent, at the bridge foot toward Southwark, both on *Mary Magdalens* day by martiall law.

8 AUG. The French Ambassador did in name of his maister the F[rench] King, made defiance vnto the King of England, and so the war began.

In the beginning of AUGUST the French [suddenly attempted Guernsey and Jersey, but were repulsed with the loss of a thousand men.]

The 16 of AUG., a man was hanged without Bishopsgate of London, and one other without Aldgate, the third at Totenham, the fourth at Waltham, and so forth in diuers other places, all by martiall law.

The rebels in Norfolke and Suffolke encamped themselues at mount Surrey, in a wood called S. *Nicholas* wood, neere vnto Norwich, against whom sir *Iohn Dudley* earle of Warwike went with an army, where bothe he and a great number of gentlemen meeting with the rebels were in such daunger, as they had thought all to haue died in that place, but God that confoundeth the purpose of all rebels, brought it so to passe, that aswel there as in all other places, they were partly by power constrained, partly by promise of their pardon, perswaded to submit themselues to their prince: the earle of Warwike entred the city of Norwich the 27 of AUGUST, when he had slaine aboue 5000. of the rebels, and taken their chief captaine *Robert Ket* of Windham [Wymondham] tanner, which might dispend in lands fifty pound [=£750 now] by yeere, and was worth in moueables aboue a thousand markes, [£666—say £10,000 now]. When he had put to execution diuers of the rebells in diuers places about Norwich, he returned.

The 28 of AUG. tidings was brought to K[ing] *Edward* and the lord protector, that the French men had taken Blacknes, Hamiltew and Newhauen by Boleine, and had slaine all the Englishmen, and taken the kings ordinance and victuals.

About this time also, a commotion began at Semer in the north-riding of Yorke-shire, and continued in the east-riding, and there ended; the principall raysers whereof were *William Ombler* of east Hesterton yeomen, *Thomas Dale* parish clearke off Semer, and *Stevenson* of Semer: being preuented by the lord president from rising at Wintringham, they drew to a place at Semer by the sea coast, and there by night rode to the beacon at Staxton, and set it on fire, and so gathered a rude route; then they went to master

Whites house, and tooke him, and *Clopton* his wiues brother, *Sauage* a merchant of Yorke, and *Bery* seruant to sir *Walter Mildmay*, which foure they murthered a mile from Semer and there lefte them naked: their number increased to 3000.

On 21 AUG. the kings pardon was offered, which *Ombler* and other refused, who were shortly after taken, and brought to York, where *Thomas Dale* and other were executed the 21 of SEPTEMBER.

[6-14 Oct. The *coup d'état* of the Earl of Warwick aided by some of the counsell and the Londoners; ending in the deposition of the Duke of Somerset as Lord Protector.]

14 OCT. The Duke of Somerset brought from Windsor and put in the Tower.

29 Nov. *Robert Ket* was hanged in chaines on the top of Norwich castle, and *William Ket* likewise hanged on the top of Windham [Wymondham] steeple.

NOV.-DEC. The Scots tooke Burticrage in Scotland, and other holds then possessed by Englishmen, where the Scots slue man, woman, and childe, except Sir *Iohn Lutterell* the captaine, whome they took prisoner.

1550 27 JAN. *Humfrey Arundell* esquire, *Thomas Holmes, Winslowe* and *Bery*, captaines of the rebels in Deuonshire, were hanged and quartered at Tyborne.

2 FEB. Candlemas Day; also Septuagesima Sunday.
  (1) 𝔗homas 𝔏eber's 𝔖ermon in the 𝔖hrouds of 𝔖t. 𝔓aul's.
  (2) The Duke of Somerset makes his Submission in the Tower.
  (3) The Lords of the Counsell are changed, Warwick's faction coming into office

6 FEB. The Duke of Somerset delivered out of the Tower.

10 FEB. One *Bel* a Suffolke man, was hanged and quartered at Tyhorne, for mouing a new rebellion in Suffolk and Essex.

16 MAR. Mid-Lent Sunday. 𝔗homas 𝔏eber's 𝔖ermon before the 𝔎ing.

31 MAR. Peace proclaimed between England and France.

8 APR. The Duke of Somerset came to court at Grenewich and was sworn of the Privy Counsell.

2 MAY. Joan of Kent was brent in Smithfield for heresie.

14 MAY. *Ric. Lion, Goddard Gorran*, and *Ric. Ireland* were executed for attempting a newe rebellion in Kent.

Trinity Terme [11 JUNE—2 JULY] was adiorned till Michaelmas, for that the gentlemen should keepe the commons from commotion.

11 JUNE. At night the high Altar in Paules Church was pulled down, and a Table set where the altar stoode, with a Vayle drawne beneath the Steppes, and on the Sundaie next [15 June] a Communion was sung at the same Table, and shortly after all the altars in London were taken downe, and Tables placed in their room.

14 DEC. Second Sunday after Advent. 𝔗homas 𝔏eber's 𝔖ermon at 𝔓auls 𝔈ross.

All these evils were by many charged to the Change of Faith. Hence the energy of the Preachers to rebut the slander, by exposing their true and many causes. The political economy of that time—faulty as we now see it to be—was based upon the principle of disinterested service for the common good. Men were urged not by their self-interest, but by the dread and love of God, to do their duty to each other and the State. Among all those preachers none more bravely fought the battle of the loyal poor; none more vigorously, even to personal hazard and danger, exposed the cruelty, covetousness, and craft of the rich and the clergy than Thomas Lever, the Cambridge Fellow, and the Boanerges of the Reformation.

BIBLIOGRAPHY.

Lever's printed Sermons were very popular when first published. No less than five editions of the three discourses were published in 1550: viz., two of the Sermon in the Shrouds, two of that before the King, and one of that at Paul's Cross.

Twenty-two years later, they were revised by Lever, and published together, under a fresh title. Since then, they have not been printed until the present edition.

One reason for this has been the excessive scarcity of copies of all these first Editions. They were soon thumbed out of existence, like the Author's *Right way from the daunger of sinne, &c.* printed at Geneva in 1556, which had all but perished by 1571: and after his death they were virtually lost in oblivion.

It may be useful therefore to quote their titles and colophons: and to distinguish the present possessors of copies, so far as I know.

ISSUES IN THE AUTHOR'S LIFETIME.

I.—*As separate publications.*

Sermon in the Shroudes of St. Paul's.

Septuagesima Sunday, 2 Feb. 1550.

∴ A dated and an undated edition.

1. TITLE. A fruitfull Sermon made in Poules churche at London in the Shroudes, the seconde daye of Febuari by Thomas Leuer. Anno M. D. and fiftie.

   COL. ¶ Imprinted at London by Iohn Daie, dwelling ouer Aldersgate, and William Seres, dwelling in Peter Colledge (∴) *Cum priuilegio ad imprimendum solum.* H. PYNE.

2. 1550. APR. 9. TITLE: as at *p.* 19.

   COL.: as at *p.* 52. H. PYNE (wants title); BODLEIAN.

Sermon before King Edward VI.

Mid-Lent Sunday, 16 March 1550.

∴ A dated and an undated edition.

3. 1550. APR. 9. TITLE, as at *p.* 53.

   COL.: as at *p.* 90. H. PYNE (T. Baker's copy); BODLEIAN.

4. 1550. TITLE. A Sermon preached the thyrd Sondaye in Lente before the Kynges Maiestie, and his honorable Counsell, by Thomas Leauer. Anno Domini. M.ccccc.l. * ∴ *

   COL. ¶ Imprynted at London by Ihon Day dwelling ouer Aldersgate, beneth saint Martyns. And are to be sold at his shop by the litle conduit in Chepesyde at the sygne of the Resurrection. *Cum priuilegio ad imprimendum solum. Per septennium.* H. PYNE.

There is a misprint in most of the title-pages. These copies have 'the thyrd Sonday in Lent,' but the text is the same. Lever took his text from 'the gospell of this day, written in the. vi. of Iohan,' see *p.* 58. This fixes the particular Sunday with absolute certainty, for in Edward VI.'s first Prayer-Book, which came into use on the Feast of Pentecost (9 June) 1549, as in our present version of it, the Miracle of Feeding the Five Thousand is the Gospell for the fourth Sunday in Lent, which fell in 1550, on 16th of March. Lever also puts the true date in the revised edition of 1572. See below.

∴ There is no authority for the above order, as regards the undated impressions. It will be seen that **1, 2** and **3** are printed by Day and Seres jointly: and **4** by Day alone.

Sermon at Paul's Cross.
Second Sunday in Advent, 14 December 1550.

5. 1550. TITLE, as at *p.* 91.
   COL., as at *p.* 144. BODLEIAN.

II.—*Collected together.*

6. 1572. FIRST TITLE. ⁋ Three fruitfull Sermons, made by Thomas Leuer. Anno domini. 1550. ⁋ And now newlie perused by the aucthour. London. *Imprinted by I. Kyngston, for Henry Kirckham.* 1572.
   TITLE TO SECOND SERMON. A Sermon preached the iiii. Sondaie in Lente, before the kynges Maiestie and his honorable Counsaile, by Thomas Leuer. Anno Domini. 1550.
   TITLE TO THIRD SERMON. A Sermon preached at Paules crosse the xiiii. daie of December, by Thomas Leuer. Anno Domini 1550.
   COL., as at *p.* 144.
      LAMBETH LIBRARY: ST. JOHN'S COLLEGE, CAMBRIDGE, (See Rev. C. H. Hartshorne's *Book Rarities of the University of Cambridge, p.* 443. Ed. 1829.)

∴ The principal variations of this edition are shown within [ ], words omitted in it that are in the earlier impressions are asterisked *. One characteristic of the revision is the prefix of *Saint* to the Apostles' names.

ISSUES SINCE THE AUTHOR'S DEATH.

I.—*Collected together.*

1870. Nov. 15. 8vo. *English Reprints:* see title at *p.* 1.

∴ Cordial thanks are due to Mr. Pyne, (who first pointed out to me the mportance of these Sermons,) for the loan,—out of his splendid collection of English Books, before 1600 A.D., of his copies of them; and to the Hon. Librarian of Lambeth Library, for permission to collate the 1572 edition.

A fruitfull Sermon made in Poules churche at London in the Shroudes the seconde daye of Februari by Thomas Leuer. Anno. M. D. and fiftie.

Od be merciful unto vs.
Good Chriſten people Chriſte Ieſu the ſonne of God, the wyſedome of the father, the ſauiour of the worlde, whyche hath redemed vs with his precious bloud moſt pitifully lamentyng our myſeries, and earneſtlye threateninge our wylfull blyndnes, cryeth oute by the voyce of the wyſe king Salomon, ſaying: *Quia uocaui, et renuiſtis. et cete. Proue. i.*[2] Becauſe I haue called (ſayeth the wyſedome of God) and ye haue denyed, I haue ſtretched forth my hand, and there was none that woulde beholde: yea ye haue diſpiſed all my councels, and [al] my rebukes haue ye not regarded, I therfore ſhall laugh at your deſtruccion, and I ſhal mocke, when it is come vpon you whiche ye haue feared. Aſſuredlye good people, God, *Qui mortem non fecit, nec lætatur in perdicione uirorum*,[3] God whiche (as the boke of wiſedome ſayth) made not death, ne dothe not delyghte in the perdicion of manne, cannot be of ſuche affeccion, as to delyghte in laughynge or mockyng our miſeries: but euen as that man whyche dothe delyghte to laughe at other mens griefes, is a man moſt farre of from lamentynge and pytyinge them to do them good: ſo is God ſo ſore offended and dyſpleaſed wyth them that diſpyſe hys counſelles, threatning or promiſes, while they might haue mercy, that he wyll as it were rather of mockyng, laughe and ſkorne, then of pitye lamente and help their miſerable wretched griefes, when as they would haue conforte. Se therfore howe mercyfully God hath called by the ſayinges and wrytinges of Moyſes, the Prophetes, and the Apoſtles, and howe fewe haue

---

[1] in the Shroudes in London. 1572. [2] Prov. *i*. 24.
[3] Wis. of Solomon, *i*. 13.

harkened to beleue. Se how wonderfully God hath ſtretched forth hys hande, in creatynge heauen and earthe, and all thynges in them conteyned, to the vſe, commoditie, and conforte to man: and how fewe do dayly behold theſe creatures, to be thankefull vnto the creatoure. Se howe muche good counſell and earneſte threatenynge God hath geuen of late vnto Englande, by ſettynge forth of his worde in the englyſhe tonge, cauſynge it to be read dayly in ye churches, to be preached purely in the pulpites, and to be rehearſed euery where in communicacion, and how many continuing, yea increaſynge their wycked lyues, regarde not gods worde, dyſpiſe his threateninges, deſyre not his mercye, feare not his vengeance.

Wythoute doute good people verye manye haue deſerued the vengeaunce of God, and yet by repentaunce founde plentye of mercye: but neuer none that euer refuſed the mercye of God hath eſcaped the vengeaunce of God in the time of hys wrathe, and furye.

Yea but what mercyes of God haue we refuſed, or what threatenynge of God haue we here in England not regarded: whyche haue forſaken the Pope, abolyſhed idolatrye and ſuperſticion, receyued goddes worde ſo gladly, reformed all thynges accordinglye therto ſo ſpedily, and haue all thinges moſt nere the order of the primitiue churche vniuerſallye? Alas good brethren, as trulye as al is not golde that glyſtereth, ſo is it not vertue and honeſty, but very vice and hipocriſie, wherof England at this day dothe moſte glorye. Wherfore the worde is playne, and the ſayinges be terryble, by the whyche at thys tyme God threateneth to punyſhe, to plage, and to deſtroy England. It is a wonderous playne worde to ſaye that Englande ſhall be deſtroyed: and vpon thys worde enſuinge, it ſhould be a terrible ſight to ſe hundred thouſandes of Scottes, Frenche menne, Papiſts, and Turkes, entryng in on euery ſyde, to murther, ſpoyle, and to deſtroye. Thys playne worde of a credyble perſon ſpoken, wyth thys terrible ſeyng afore our eyes in ſight [our iyes in prefence,] wold make oure corage to fall, and oure hertes to ryue in peces, for wofull forowe, feare, and heauineffe.

Alas England, God, whom thou mayeft beleue for his truthe, hathe fayd playnly thou fhalt be deftroyed, and all thyne ennemyes, bothe Scots, Frenchmen, Papiftes, and Turkes, I do not meane the men in whome is fome mercye, but the moft cruell vices of thefe thy enemyes beynge wythout all pitie, as the couetoufenes of Scotland, the pryde of Fraunce, the hipocryfy of Rome, and the Idolatrye of the Turkes. A hundred thoufande of thefe enemies are landed at thy hauens, haue entred thy fortes, and do procede to fpoyle, murther, and vtterly deftroy : and yet for all this thou wretched Englande beleueft not gods worde, regardeft not hys threatninge, calleft not for mercye, ne fearefte not gods vengeaunce. Wherfore God beinge true of hys word, and righteous in hys dedes, thou Englande whyche wylt haue no mercye, fhalt haue vengeaunce, whyche wylte not be faued, fhalte be deftroyed. For God hath fpoken, and it is wrytten.

Omne regnum in fediuifum defolabitur.[1] Euerye kyngdome that is deuyded in it felfe, fhall be defolate, and deftroyed. And Salomon fayeth : Becaufe they haue hated learnyng and not receiued the feare of God, deftruccion commeth fodaynlye : Yea trulye, and bryngeth Idolaters vnto mifery, and proude men vnto fhame. Ye all here fele, fee, knowe, and haue experience, howe that this Realme is deuyded in it felfe by opynyons in relygyon, by rebellious fedicion, yea and by couetoufe ambicion, euerye manne pullynge and halynge towardes them felues, one from another.

It is not onelye diuyded, but alfo rente, torne, and plucked cleane in pieces. Yea and euerye couetoufe manne is an Idolater, fettynge that mynd and loue vpon ryches, whyche oughte to be geuen vnto God onely.

Euery couetoufe man hateth learnynge, and receyueth not the feare of God, for the gredy defire that he hathe to the lucre of thys worlde. Euerye couetoufe man is proude, thynkynge hymfelfe more worthy a

[1] Matt. *xii.* 25.

pounde, then a nother man a penye, more fitte to haue
chaunge of fylkes and veluettes, then other to haue
bare frife cloth, and more conueniente for hym to haue
aboundaunce of diuerfe dilicates for hys daintye toth,
then for other to haue plenty of biefes and muttons for
theyr hongry bellyes: and finnally that he is more
worthye to haue gorgeoufe houfes to take his pleafure
in, in bankettynge, then laborynge men to haue poore
cotages to take reſt in, in flepynge. Vndoubtedlye
God wyll make all thofe to fall wyth fhame, which fet
them felues vp in pryde fo hygh, that they can not fee
other men to be chyldren of the fame heauenlye father,
heires of the fame kingdome, and bought wyth the
fame pryce of Chriſtes bloude, that they take them
felues to be. That realme, that realme that is full of
couetoufnes, is full of diuifion, is full of contempt of
goddes mercye, yea and fclaunder of hys worde, is full
of Idolatry and is full of pryde. Diuifion is a figne of
deſtruccion, contemning of goddes mercye caufeth his
vengeaunce to come fodeynly: Idolatrye euer endeth
in mifery, and pryde neuer efcapeth fhame. Then if
you fele, knowe, and haue experyence, that Englande
by reafon of couetoufnes is full of diuifion, is full of
contempte of goddes mercye, is full of Idolatrye, is
full of pryde, Flatter not your felues in youre owne
phan[ta]fies, but beleue the word of God, whiche telleth
you truelye that Englande fhall be deſtroyed fodainly,
miferably, and fhamefullye. The fame deſtruccion
was tolde to the Sodomites, was tolde to the Niniuites: was deferued of the Sodomites, and was deferued of the Niniuites: but came vpon the Sodomites,
and was tourned from the Niniuytes. And why? For
becaufe the Sodomytes regarded not goddes threatenynges and were plaged wyth gods vengeaunce, the
Niniuytes regarded goddes threatnynges, and efcaped
gods vengeaunce.

Now all you Englyfhe men at the reuerence of God,
for the tender mercyes of Iefu Chriſt, for the reuerent
loue to youre moſt gentle and gracious kynge, for the

fauegarde of your cuntry, and for tender pyty of your owne wiues, your children, and your felues, caufe not Englande to bee deftroyed wyth gods vengeaunce, as was the Cytie of the Sodomites: but repent, lament and amend your liues, as did the good Niniuites. For if ye fpedely repent, and myferably [and pitifully] lamente, and be afhamed of your vainglory, couetoufnes, and ambicion, ye fhal caufe couetous, fedicious, proude, and vicious England, fodenly, miferablye yea and fhamefully in the fyghte and iudgement of the world, to vanyfh away. And fo finne and abhominacion deftroyed by the repentaunce of man, this pleafaunte place of Englande, and good people fhall be preferued and faued by thy [the] mercy of God. For els if man wil not forfake his fynne, God wyll not fpare to deftroye both the man and hys place with his fynne.

Wherefore the Epyftle by the order nowe taken, appoynted for thys fourth Sunday after twelfe tyde, is a leffon moft mete to teache you to knowe and lamente youre greuous finnes of late committed, whyche as
yet be in fuche cafe, that man wythout
greate repentaunce cannot fone amende
them, nor god of hys ryghteoufnes
much longer fuffer them. It is
written in the beginning
of the.[x]iii. Chap. of
Paul to the Rom.
on this wyfe.

Verye foule be fubiecte vnto the hygher powers, for there is no power but of God. Thofe powers whych be, are ordeyned of God. Wherefore he that refyfteth power, refyfteth the ordinaunce of God, but they whyche doo refifte, fhall receyue to themfelues iudgement. For Rulers are not to be feared for good doinges, but for euil. Wouldeft thou not feare the power? do that whiche is good, and thou fhalt haue praife of it. But if thou do euyll, feare: for he beareth not the fweard wythout a caufe, for he is the minifter of God to auenge in wrath, hym that doeth euyl.

Wherefore ye muſt nedes be fubiecte, not only for wrathe, but alfo for confcience fake. For thys do ye paye tribute: For they are the miniſters of God attendyng to thys fame thynge. Geue therefore vnto euery one ducties: tribute to whome trybute is due, cuſtome to whome cuſtum is due, feare to whom feare is due, honoure to whom honoure is due.

Thus haue ye heard howe that euery one oughte to be vnder obedience, and geue vnto other that whych is due. Howbeit experience declareth howe that here in Englande pore men haue been rebels, and ryche men haue not done their ductie. Bothe haue done euyll to prouoke goddes vengeance, neyther doth repente to procure gods mercye.

Nowe for the better vnderſtandyng of thys matter, here in thys texte, fyrſt is to be noted, how that *Anima*, the foule, for as muche as it is the chiefe parte of man, is taken for the whole man: as we in oure englyſhe tonge, take the bodye beynge the worfe part for the whole. As if I faye, euery bodye here, I meane euerye man or woman here. So in the fourthe of Leuiti. *Anima quæ peccauerit, ipfa moritur.*[1] The foule that finneth, it fhall dye: meanyng the man or woman that fynneth. And euen fo here Paule by the Ebrue phrafe and maner of fpeche, commaundeth euery foule, whych is by the englifhe phrafe euery bodye, that is to faye, euerye perfon, man, woman, and child to be fubiect. As thou art in dede, fo acknowledge thy felfe in thine own mynde *Hypotaffeſtho* [ὑποτασσέσθαι], yat is to faye, fet or placed vnder the hygher powers, yea and that by God. For as there is no power of authorithy but of god, fo is there none put in fubieccion vnder theym but by God. Thofe powers whiche be are ordeyned of God. As is the power of the father euer hys chyldren of the hufband ouer hys wyfe, of the mafter ouer hys feruauntes, and of the kynge ouer hys

[1] Ezek. xviii. 4.

lande and fubiectes: wyth all kynde of magiftrates in their offices ouer their charge.

Nowe to proue that thefe bee the ordinaunces of God, we haue by goddes word bothe in the olde teftamente and in the newe, their names rehearfed, theyr offices dyfcribed, and theyr duties [duetie] commaunded. Yet that* notwythftandynge fome there be that labour by wreftynge of the fcripture to pulle them felues from vnder due obedience: faiynge that it appeareth in the actes of the Apoftles how that they hadde all thynges commen, and therfore none more goodes or ryches, power or aucthoritie, then other, but all alyke.

Truthe it is, that the Apoftles had all thynges comen, yea and that chriften men, in that they are chriften men rather then couetous men, haue all thynges comen, euen vnto thys day. How be it ther can be nothyng more contrarye or further difagreyng from that phantaftical commenneffe, or rather from that diuelyfhe diforder, and vnrighteoufe robry [robberie], where as Idle lubbers myghte lyue of honefte mennes laboures, then to haue all thynges comen as the Apoftles hadde, as chriften men haue, and as I do meane. And thys is theyr vfage, and my meanynge: that ryche menne fhoulde kepe to theym felues no more then they nede, and geue vnto the poore fo muche as they nede. For fo Paule wryteth to the Corinthes. I meane not (faythe Paull, fpeakynge to the ryche) to haue other fo eafed, that you therby fhoulde be brought in trouble of nede, but after an indif[fe]renc[i]e, that at this tyme your abundaunce, myght helpe their nede.

And fo dyd the Apoftles take order as appeareth in the fourth of the actes. *Quotquot habebant agros et poffeffiones. etc.*[1] As many as hadde landes and poffeffions dyd fell them, and broughte the prices vnto the feete of the Apoftles, and diuifion was made vnto euerye one accordinge vnto euerye mannes neede. So they whyche myght fpare dydde frelye geue, and they whiche hadde nede dyd thankefully receyue.

For fo is it [it is] mete, that chriften mens goodes fhuld

[1] Acts *iv.* 34.

be comen vnto euery mans nede, and priuate to no mans lufte. And thofe [thefe] comune goodes to bee difpofed by liberall geuers, and not fpoyled by gredy catchers. So that euery man may haue accordyng to hys nede fufficient, and not accordynge to hys fpoyle fo muche as he can catche, no nor accordyng to the value of the thyng, euerye man a penye, a grote, or a fhyllyng. For they that Imagyne, couet, or wyfhe to haue all thynges comune, in fuche forte that euerye man myght take what hym lufte, wolde haue all thynges comen and open vnto euerye mans lufte, and nothynge referued or kept for any mans nede. And they that wolde haue like quantitie of euery thyng to be geuen to euerye man, entendyng therby to make all alyke, do vtterly deftroy the congregacyon, the mifticall bodye of Chryft, wheras there muft nedes be dyuers members in diuerfe places, hauynge diuerfe duetyes. For as [fainct] Paul fayth: yf all the bodye be an eye, where is then hearyng? or yf all be an eare, where is then fmellyng? meanyng therby, that yf all be of one forte, eftate, and roume in the comen wealth, how can then dyuerfe duetyes of diuerfe neceffarye offices be done?

So that the fre herte, and liberall gyfte of the ryche, muft make all that he may fpare, comen to releue the nede of the poore: yea yf there be great neceffitye, he muft fell both landes and goodes, to maynteyne charitie: And thus to haue all thinges comen, doth derogate or take away nothynge from the authoritye of rulers. But to wyll to haue all thynges comen, in fuche forte that idle lubbers (as I fayde) myghte take and wafte the geines of laborers wythout reftraint of authoritie, or to haue lyke quantitye of euerye thynge to be geuen to euery man, is vnder a pretence to mende al, purpofely to marre all. For thofe fame men pretendinge to hate [haue] couetoufnes, wold be as rych as the rycheft: and fayinge that they hate pryde, wold be as hyghly taken as the beft, and femynge to abhorre enuye, can not be content[ed] to fe any other rycher or better then they them felues be. Now I heare fome faye that

thys errour is the fruyte of the fcripture in englyfhe.
No, neyther thys, nor no other erroure commeth becaufe the fcripture is fet forth in the englyfhe tonge, but
becaufe the rude people lackynge the counfell of learned
menne to teache theim the trewe meanynge when they
reade it, or heare it, mufte nedes folowe theyr owne
Imaginacion in takynge of it. And the chiefeft caufe
that maketh them to imagine thys abhominable errour,
that there fhuld be no ryche menne nor rulers, cum-
meth becaufe fome ryche men and rulers (marke that I
faye fome, for all bee not fuche) but I faye fome ryche
men, and rulers by the abufe of their ryches and aucthoritye, dothe more harme then good vnto the comen
wealth, and more griefe then confort vnto the people.
For nowe a dayes ryche menne and rulers do catche,
purcheffe, and procure vnto them felues great commodities from many men, and do fewe and fmall pleafures vnto any men.

As for example of ryche men, loke at the merchauntes of London, and ye fhall fe, when as by their
honeft vocacion, and trade of marchandife god hath
endowed them with great abundaunce of ryches, then
can they not be content with the profperous welth
of that vocacion to fatiffye theym felues, and to helpe
other, but their riches mufte abrode in the countrey
to bie fermes out of the handes of worfhypfull gentlemen, honefte yeomen, and pore laborynge hufbandes.
Yea nowe alfo to bye perfonages, and benefices, where
as they do not onelye bye landes and goodes, but alfo
lyues and foules of men, from God and the comen
wealth, vnto the deuyll and theim felues. A myf-
cheuoufe marte of merchandrie is this, and yet nowe fo
comenly vfed, that therby fhepeheardes be turned to
theues, dogges into wolues, and the poore flocke of
Chrift, redemed wyth his precious bloud, mofte miferablye pylled, and fpoyled, yea cruelly deuoured. Be
thou marchaunt of the citye, or be thou gentleman in
the contrey, be thou lawer, be you courtear, or what
maner of man foeuer thou be, that can not, yea yf

thou be mafter doctor of diuinitie, that wyl not do thy duety, it is not lawfull for the to haue perfonage, benefice, or any fuche liuyng, excepte thou do fede the flocke fpiritually wyth goddes worde, and bodelye wyth honefte hofpitalitye. I wyll touch diuerfe kyndes of ryche men and rulers, that ye maye fe what harme fome of theim do wyth theyr ryches and authoritye. And efpeciallye I wyll begynne wyth theym that be beft learned, for they feme belyke to do mofte good wyth ryches and authoritie vnto theim committed. If I therefore beynge a yonge fimple fcholer myghte be fo bolde, I wolde afke an aunciaent, wyfe, and well learned doctor of diuinitie, whych cometh not at hys benefice, whether he were bounde to fede hys flocke in teachynge of goddes worde, and kepyng hofpitalitie or no? He wold anfwere and faye: fyr my curate fupplieth my roume in teachynge, and my farmer in kepynge of houfe. Yea but mafter doctor by your leaue, both thefe more for your vauntage then for the paryfhe conforte: and therfore the mo fuche feruauntes that ye kepe there, the more harme is it for your paryfhe, and the more fynne and fhame for you. Ye may thynke that I am fumwhat faucye to laye fynne and fhame to a doctor of diuinitie in thys folemne audience, for fome of theim vfe to excufe the matter, and faye: Thofe whych I leaue in myne abfence do farre better then I fhoulde do, yf I taryed there my felfe.

Nowe good mafter doctor ye faye the verye truthe, and therfore be they more worthye to haue the benefice then you your felfe, and yet neyther of you bothe fufficient mete, or able: they for lacke of habilitye, and you for lacke of good wyll. Good wyll quod he? Naye I wolde wyth all my harte, but I am called to ferue the kynge in other places, and to take other offices in the comen wealthe. Heare then what I fhall aunfwere yet once agayne: There is lyuynges and rewardes due and belongyng to theim that labour in thofe offyces, and fo oughte you to be contente

wyth the lyuyng and reward of that office onelye, and
take no more, the duetye of the whyche office by your
labour and diligence ye can difcharge onlye, and do
no more. And fo Paule wryteth vnto the Corrinth.
fayinge: The Lord hathe ordeyned that they whyche
preache the Gofpell, fhulde lyue vpon the Gofpell.[1]
And vnto the T[h]effalonians. He that dothe not
labour fhulde not eate.[2]

By thefe textes well fet together, you may conclude
and learne, that there as you beftowe your labour, there
maye ye take a lyuynge, and ther as ye beftowe no
labour, there ought ye to take no liuyng. Well let vs
procede further vnto other nowe, for I perceyue that
all that which I haue fpoken againft them that take
greate geynes of theyr benefices, and do lytle good to
theyr benefice, maye feme to be fpoken agaynft the
vniuerfityes, yea and againft the kynges mayeftye:
whyche now by reafon of improperacions haue no lytle
geynes of benefices, and yet beftowe no great laboure
nor almes vpon the paryfhioners of thofe benefices.
Surely, for as muche as I feare the vengeaunce of God
more yf I fhoulde not fpeake the truthe, then the difpleafure of man yf he be offended in hearynge of the
truth, trulye I wyll tell you. Seyng that improperacions beynge fo euyll that no man can alowe theym,
be nowe fo employed vnto the vniuerfities, yea and
vnto the yerelye reuenues of the kynges maieftye, that
fewe dare fpeake agaynft them, ye maye fe that fome
men, not onelye by the abufe of ryches and authoritie,
but alfo by the abufe of wyfedom and pollicie do much
harme, and fpecially thofe, by whofe meanes thys realme
is nowe brought into fuch cafe that eyther learnyng in
the vniuerfitie, and neceffarye reuenues belongynge to
the mofte hygh authoritye is lyke to decaye, or elles
improperacions to be maynteined, whyche bothe be fo
deuyllyfheandabhominable that yf eyther of them come
to effecte, it wyll caufe the vengeaunce of God vtterly
to deftroy this realme. Do not thynke that I meane

[1] 1 Cor. ix. 14.   [2] 2 Thess. iii. 10.

any thyng agaynſt that whyche the kynges mayeſtye by acte of Parliament hathe done: no nor that I wyll couer in fcilence, or alowe by flatterie that whyche couetoufe officers (fome as I fuppofe nowe beyng prefente) contrarye to goddes lawes, the kynges honour, and the comen wealth vfe to do. For in fuppreſſinge of Abbeyes, Cloyſters, Colleges, and Chauntries, the entente of the kynges maieſtie that dead is, was, and of this our kynge now, is verye godlye, and the purpofe or els the pretence of other, wonderoufe goodlye: that therby fuche abundaunce of goodes as was fuperſticiouſly fpente vpon vayne ceremonies, or voluptuouſly vpon idle bellies, myght come to the kynges handes to beare hys great charges, neceffarilie beſtowed in the comen wealthe, or partly vnto other mennes handes, for the better releue of the pore, the mayntenaunce of learning, and the fettinge forth of goddes worde. Howe be it couetoufe officers haue fo vfed thys matter, that euen thofe goodes whyche dyd ferue to the releue of the poore, the mayntenaunce of learnyng, and to confortable neceffary hofpitalitie in ye comen wealth, be now turned to maynteyne worldly, wycked couetoufe ambicion.

I tell you, at the fyrſte the intente was verie godly, the pretence wonderoufe goodly, but nowe the vfe or rather the abufe and myforder of thefe thynges is worldlye, is wycked, is deuilyſhe, is abhominable.

The kynge maye haue, and wolde to God he hadde in hys handes to beſtowe better, all that was euell* mifpente vpon fuperſticious Ceremonies, and voluptuous Idle bellyes.

But you whych haue gotten thefe goodes into your own* handes, to turne them from euyll to worfe, and other goodes mo frome good vnto euyll, be ye fure it is euen you that haue offended God, begyled the kynge, robbed the ryche, fpoyled the pore, and brought a comen wealth into a comen miferye. It is euen you, that muſt eyther be plaged with gods vengeaunce as wer the Sodomytes, or amende by repentaunce as did the Nineuites. Euen you it is that muſt eyther make reſtitucion and amendes ſpedely, or elles fele the vengeaunce of God greuouſly. Do not thynke that by reſtitucion and amendes makyng I meane the buyldynge agayne of abbeyes or cloyſters, no I do not: For yf charitable almes, honeſte hoſpitalitie, and neceſſary ſcholes, for the bryngynge vp of yougth had ben indifferently maynteyned and not cleane taken away in ſome places, I woulde not at this time haue ſpoken of reſtitucion. Howe be it ſure I am, that if at* the orderinge of theſe thynges there had been in the officers as much godlines as there was couetouſnes, ſuperſticious men had not bene put from their liuinges to their penſions out of thoſe houſes, wher they myght haue had ſchole maſters to haue taught them to be good, and for leſſe wages: or for the reſeruacion of their penſions, receyued into cures, and perſonages, where as they can do no good, and wyll do muche harme. Here as concerninge theſe thinges I ſaye, if man do not make reſtitucion, God wyll take vengeaunce. For the people that by thys meanes contynue in deuelyſhe ſuperſticion, and begyn vngracious rebellion, do dye, and are damned in their owne ſynnes, but the bloud of their bodyes and ſoules ſhall be required at youre handes. Yea and the abhominable errour of thoſe that would haue no rulers in authoritie, cometh partelye by your occaſion, whyche vnto your owne vayne glorye, and pryuate commoditie [priuate authoritie], do abuſe the power and authoritie ordeyned of God to hys glorye, and to the commen wealthe. Thus ye perceyue howe that ſome ryche menne and rulers abuſynge their ryches and authoritie, do make ſome eyther to iudge that it ſhoulde be farre better then it is, if there were neyther riche men nor rulers: Howbeit thoſe men are farre deceyued. And Paule telleth the truth, ſayinge that thoſe which be, are ordeyned of God.

Then ſome wyll aſke thys queſtyon: Seynge there is

no euyll of God, howe can euyll rulers or officers be of God? You honeſte men that be here, and dwell in the countrey, heare this leſſon, and marke it, and take it home wyth you, for your ſelues, and your neyghbour. It is God, *Qui facit hypocrita regnare propter peccata populi.* It is God, as the ſcripture in the xxxiiii. of Iob doth teſtifye, whych maketh an hypocritie to be a ruler for the ſynnes of the people. Nowe the people of the countrey vſe to ſaye, that their gentlemen and officers were neuer ſo full of fayre woordes and euyll dedes (whych is hypocrify) as they nowe be. For a gentleman wyl ſaye that he loueth his tenaunt as well as hys father dyd, but he kepeth not ſo good a houſe to make them chere as hys father dyd, and yet he taketh mo fynes, and greater rentes to make them neadye, then hys father hadde.

Another wyll ſay that he would bye a Lordſhyppe of the kyng, for the loue that he hath to the tenauntes thereof, but aſſone as he hathe boughte it, by takynge of fynes, heyghnyng of rentes, and ſellyng away of commodities, he maketh the ſame tenantes pay for it. Another ſayth that he would haue an office to do good in hys contrey, but as ſone as he hath authoritie to take the fee to hym ſelfe, he ſetteth hys ſeruaunte to do hys duetye, and in ſtede of wages he geueth them authoritie to lyue of pyllage, brybry and extorcion in the countrey.

Now you of the countrey, marke your leſſon I ſaye, and take it home wyth you. It is God that maketh theſe euyl men to be gentlemen rulers, and officers in the countrey: it is the ſinnes of the people that cauſeth God to make theſe men youre rulers. The man is ſometymes euyll, but the authoritie from God is alwayes good, and God geueth good authoritye vnto euyll men, to punyſhe the ſynnes of the euyll people. It is not therefore repynyng, rebellyng, or reſiſtyng gods ordinance, that wyll amende euyll rulers. For [ſainct] Paule ſayeth, that all powers be of goddes ordinaunce. And in Iob it is playne, that euyll menne bee made rulers by God: So that who foeuer refyfteth the offycers, be the menne neuer fo euyll that be in office, he refifteth the ordinaunce of God, he can not preuayle againfte God, but furely he fhall be plaged of God. And as the people can haue no remedye againft euyll rulers by rebellyon, fo can the rulers haue no redreffe of rebellious people by oppreffyon. Example of bothe we haue in the thyrd booke of Kynges, where as it appeareth that Roboam leauyng good counfell to vfe the people wyth gentlenes and folowyng euyll counfell to kepe them vnder by extremytye, dyd fo exafperate and ftyrre vp the hertes of the people againft him beyng their kyng, that ten partes of them dyd by fedicious rebellion, burfte oute from hym, and were neuer after fubiecte vnto hym, nor to none of his pofteritie. And thofe rebellious people by Ieroboam whom they them felues chofe to be their kynge, or rather the captayne of theyr rebellyon, were brought into farre worfe cafe and more myferye then euer they were afore, compelled to forfake God, and to vfe Idolatrye, and were euer after plaged wyth fodeyne deathe, honger, dearthe, warres, captyuytie, and all kynde of myferye.

Learne therefore ye people if ye inforce to eafe your felues, wheras ye imagine that ye be euyll entreated of men, be ye fure that ye fhall fele in deede that ye fhall be more greuouflye afflycted by the ordynaunce of God. And learne ye rulers if ye intende by onely fuppreffion to kepe vnder rebellion, be ye fure if ye thrufte it downe in one place it wyll brafte out wyth more vyolence and greater daunger in ten other places, to the further dyfquietynge of you beynge rulars, and to the vtter deftruccyon of all youre people beynge rebelles.

Heare ye people what God fayeth by thofe people that wyll not be in fubieccion, becaufe they thynke the men to be euyl whiche be in authoritye. Yea harke what the Lord fayeth as concernynge the proude, ambycyoufe, and vncyrcumcyfed Kynge Nabugodonozer whyche was an euyll manne in dede, in the twentie and feuen Chapter of Hieremye. *Gens et regnum, et cetera.*[1]

That people and realme that doth not ferue Nabugodonezer ye kinge of Babilon, and whofoeuer putteth not his necke vnder the yocke of Nabugodnozer the kynge of Babilon, I (fayeth the Lorde) wyl vifet vpon that people in fweard, honger, and in peftylence. And in the xxvii. of the fame Prophete. *Catenas ligneas contriuifti, et facies pro eis [catenas] ferreas.*[2] Thou haft broken the fetters of wood, and fhalt make for them fetters of yron. By the whiche he declareth yat as a pryfoner in ye kepynge of a gayler, if he breake hys fetters of wood, fhall not therefore by the gayler be fet at lybertye, but rather cheyned wyth more ftronge fetters of yron: Euen fo, people beynge in the kepyng of God, if they by rebellyon breake their yocke of fubieccion, whych they nowe haue, fhall not therfore by God be putte at libertie, but rather be thrufte into a more ftraite, greuous, and ftronger yocke, where they fhall be fure neuer to haue libertie nor eafe.

Wherfore ye people, if ye fele your burden is heauye, and your yocke greuoufe, pacyently fuffer, and call vnto the Lorde: for then he wyll heare thee, and he wyl relieue thee, and he wyll delyuer thee.

And you rulers, becaufe ye knowe that the people oughte not to forfake or refufe what burden or yoke fo euer ye charge them wyth all, fee that ye charge them with no more then they maye beare and fuffer. For if they cry vnto you for reliefe and eafemente, and you wyll not regarde theyr forowes, but imagynynge that they be to wealthy, ye wyll encreafe their miferye, and decay their wealthe, as Pharao, and Roboam dyd: Well then, if the examples of Pharao and Roboam wyll not fuffyce you, marcke what God, by the prophet Ezechi. fayth (I pray you) in the. xxxiiii. of Ezechiel, *Audite paftores. &c.*[3] Do not thynke that for becaufe paftors be named there, yat therfore it is al fpoken onely vnto the clargye, but for afmuche as all officers and rulers ought rather to be feders then fpoilers, it is

---

[1] Jer. xxvii. 8.   [2] Jer. xxviii. 13.   [3] Ezek. xxxiv. 8.

spoken vnto you officers, which do not enter in by ye dore
of loue, as the shephearde to feede, but clime ouer another
awaye [an other waie] thorowe couetousnes as a thiefe,
to robbe and spoyle the flocke of Christ in your office.
Here what the Lorde sayeth vnto you officers yat fede
youre selues by seking of gaines, and not your flocke
by doing your dutie. Thus sayth the Lord: I my selfe
wyl vp on these pastors, and I wil require my shepe at
their handes, and wyll make them to ceafe from fedyng
of my flocke, yea the pastors shal fede them selues no
more, for I wyll delyuer my flocke out of their handes,
and they shall be no longer a praye for them to fede
vpon. Vndoubtedly if ye shuld entende by your authority rather your selues to liue in riote, then to kepe ye
people in quietnes, your rulynge shulde not longe continue. Surely ther is none other remedy for ryche or
poore, high or low, gentleman or yeoman, to helpe to
amende the disquietnes in thys realme, but to pulle
and rote that* out of youre hertes, which is roted in
euery one of your hertes, the rote of all euyll, whyche
is couetousnes. For euen you husbandmen whyche
crye out vpon the couetousnes of gentlemen and
officers, it is euen couetousnes in you, yat causeth,
and ingendreth couetousnes in them. For, for to get
your neyghbours ferme, ye wyll offer and disire them
to take bribes, fynes, and rentes more then they loke
for, or then you your selues be wel able to pay. It
is a wonderous thing to se gentlemen take so great
rentes, fynes, and ingressaunce for couetousnes to ad-
uaunce theyr owne landes: Howebeit it is a farre more
wonderfull thyng to see husbande men offer and geue
so greate fynes, rentes, incomes, yea and bribes for
couetousnes to gette other mennes fermes. It semeth
to come of great couetousnes for riche men, to make
strayte lawes to saue their owne goodes: Howebeit it
is in deede a farre more couetousnes for poore men by
rebellion to robbe, and spoile other mens goodes. And
this dare I saye, takyng all you to beare recorde, that
the forest lawes that euer any tyraunt made in any

lande, if they fhuld continue many yeares coulde not caufe fuch and fo great murther, myfchiefe, and wretchednes as ye perceyue and know that thys rebellyon in England contynuynge but a fewe monethes, hath caufed: by the which ye may learne that althoughe lawers be comenly called moft couetous, yet compare them with rebels, and as pickinge theft, is leffe then murtheryng robrye [robberie]: fo is the couetoufnes of gredy lawers which begyle craftely, farleffe then the couetoufnes of rebelles, whych fpoyle cruelly. Lette vs therefore euerye one acknoweledgynge our owne fautes, where as moft euyll fpryngeth, there laboure fyrfte wyth mofte diligence to plucke vp the roote of that euil, whyche is couetoufnes : that God ingraftynge grace in vs, maye geue occafyon vnto oure Rulars rather to bee occupyed in rewardynge of vertue, then in punyfheyng of vyce: Yea that God be not prouoked by our finnes to fende euyll rulers to punyfhe euyll men, but rather moued by oure repentaunce, to preferue thefe good rulers whiche be fente alreadye to the greate comfort of all good men : efpecially the kinges maiefty, whofe godlynes, vertue, and grace, is lyke to make this realme to floryfhe, if oure fynnes do not caufe God to thinke our realme vnworthy to enioye the treafure of fo precyous a Iewell. Manye other noble men therebe as I trufte, fome that I do certaynlye knowe, whofe tender heartes do muche lamente youre griefes, and whofe godlye prouifion wyll be muche vnto youre comforte, if your vnpaciente ftubburnes do not difapoynte their good purpofe. If euer at any tyme God did fend vnto any afflycted people releyfe, comforte, and profperytye, it came alwayes by good rulers, at fuch tyme as the people beeynge in afflyccyon, dyd humble them felues in pacyence, and cryed vnto the Lorde wyth prayer, as is apparente in the houndreth and feuen Pfalme. *Clamauerunt ad dominum cum tribularentur, et de neceffitatibus eorum liberauit eos.*[1] When they were in trouble they called vnto thee [the] Lorde, and he de-

---

[1] Ps. cvii. 13.

liuered them forth of their troubloufefome gryefes.
And in the bookes of the iudges and of the kynges, ye
maye reade how that God, to delyuer his people forth
of miferye, and to profper them in wealth, dyd reyfe
vp good rulers as Gedeon, Barac, Iepthe, Sampfon,
Dauid, Samuel, and fuche other. And wythoute
doubte euen at this time here in England, God
hathe rayfed vp a gracyous kynge, and fome fuche
noble men as be neyther cruell nor couetous. If
ther be therfore in vs pacience, humility, thankfulnes, and prayer, furelye we fhall foone feele relyefe,
conforte and profperitie.

Thei therfore yat as yet feele them felues greued,
let them cal vnto ye lord, lokinge for his helpe in
paciente fuffering, not prouoking his vengeaunce by
vngracious rebellinge agaynfte hys officers, vnhappye
refifting hys ordinaunce: vnhappy refiftyng may I well
call it, for vnhappye are all they that vfe it, purchafing
thereby to them felues iudgement, vengeaunce, and
damnacyon. O howe vnhappye haue they been here
in England, whiche haue not quietlye fuffered a confortable reformacion of their greateft griefes and
harmes, to procede from god to them by his ordinaunce, but vnpacientlye grudginge haue offended
god, difquieted this realm, and vndone them felues,
by refyftynge goddes ordynaunce. For the greateft
griefe that hathe been vnto the people in thys realme,
hath bene the inclofing of comens, as concernyng
the whyche the powers ordeyned of GOD for that
purpofe, made an acte of parlyamente, forbiddynge
anye man to enclofe vnto hys pryuate vfe, that whyche
of long tyme had bene taken, and vfed as common.
And afterwardes, the fame powers dyd fende forthe
proclamacions, warnynge theym whyche contrarye to
thys acte of parliament had inclofed groundes, offend-
ynge the people, that they accordynge to thefe Proclamacions fhoulde laye the fame inclofed landes
abroade agayne, to fatyffye the acte of parliamente,
and to releue the people. And for becaufe neyther of

these wayes toke effecte, there was immediatly further commiſſions dyrected to put ſuche men in authoryty, as could eaſelye, and woulde gladly, and were purpoſed ſpedely to haue layed vnlawfull incloſed landes abrode agayne, in ſuch quiet ſorte as ſhoulde haue bene moſt to the kynges honour, to ye wealth of thys realme, and to the greateſt comforte of thoſe whyche were moſt greued. Now howe the people dyd take or rather how they dyd reſyſte and wythſtand thys, ye know.

And I ſhall rehearſe whan as I haue telled you of one other thyng whyche beynge of longer contynuance in Englande, hath done ferre more harme, and yet the gryef therof fer leſſe, yea nothynge at all felt. For the deadely wound therof dyd brynge the people paſt all felynge of gryefe. And the venomous poyſen broughte the people in ſuche a Maze, that they dyd not ſele and perceyue them ſelues to be in moſt horryble myſerable wretchednes, whan as the worde of GOD, the breade of lyfe, the ſauyng health in Chriſt Ieſu, was taken a way, and in a ſtraunge language ſhut, and cloſed vp from theym, ſo that they wythout felyng were led from God by mannes tradicions vnto vayne ceremonis, to be moſt venemouſly poyſoned wyth dyueliſhe ſuperſticion. Therefore whan as the mercyfull goodnes of God beholdyng the miſeries of the people, by the prouydence of the kynges maieſtye, and his counſell, purpoſely ordeined of God to conforte, healpe, and amend the people of thys realme, by the reſtoryng of goddes worde, and ſettynge it playnelye forthe in the Englyſh tong, with the ryght vſe and dew adminiſtracion of hys ſacramentes to be imprynted, and confyrmed in our hartes: Whan as I ſaye, by theſe gracyous meanes, and godlye order, God hym ſelfe dyd offer vnto the people, relyefe, comforte, and proſperitye: Then the vngodlye, vngracious and vnhappye people, beynge mooſte vnkynde, where as they ſhoulde haue bene mooſte thankefull, dyſtruſted GOD, dyſpiſed hys ordinaunce, and preſumed of theyr owne wylfulnes fo farre as they coulde or myghte, to wythftand the ordynaunce of God, refufed the grace of God, and procured to theym felues the vengeaunce of God. Wherfore we hauynge thys terrible example in frefh memorye, and feynge a gracyous Kyng, and Godly rulars ordeyned of GOD, to amende oure gryefes, althoughe all that cannot be amended in one day, whyche hath bene appayryng manye yeres, yet let vs pacientlye fuffer for a tyme, not doubtynge but that that reliefe, comforte, and wealth, whyche God hathe promyfed vnto Englande by hys word, offered of hys goodnes, and begon by his ordinaunce, fhalbe brought vnto paffe, by hys wyfdome and myghte: in fuche wyfe as fhall be mofte for hys glorye, the kynges honoure, the wealth of the realme, and moft to the conforte of theym that moofte pacyentlye in hope, trufte to [in] goddes goodnes. Thefe examples haue I rehearfed to teach you as it were by experience, howe true this faying of [faincte] Paul is: They whyche wythftande or refyfte the powers ordeyned of God, receyue vnto them felues Iudgemente: whyche is vengeaunce, and damnacion. Let vs therfore amend our lyues, and be good men, and we fhall not nede to hate and feare, but haue greate occafion to loue, and trufte thofe whyche be nowe our chyefe rulars. For they be as [S.] Paule fayeth, made rulars, not to put theym in feare that do good, but theym whyche do euyll: fo that none nedeth to feare thefe rulers, but euell doers. Whyche in euyll doynge haue deferued of the rulers to be punyfhed, and in refyftynge theyr power ordeyned of GOD, do haften, and aggrauate towardes theym felues, the fore vengeaunce of GOD. It foloweth: Wouldeft thou be wythout feare of power, do that whyche is good, and thou fhalte haue prayfe of it: for he is the mynyfter of God to do the[e] good, but yf thou do euyl, feare. For he beareth not the fwearde wythout a caufe, but is the mynifter of GOD to aduenge in wrath hym that doeth euyll.

All thefe wordes [fainct] Peter concludeth bryefelye in

the second of hys fyrſt Epiſtle, ſaying that thoſe that haue rule and authorytye, be ſente *ad vindictam malorum, laudem vero bonorum*.[1] That is to ſaye: to take vengeaunce of euell doers, and to commende the good.

Whoſoeuer thou arte therefore and of whatſoeuer degree or ſorte thou bee. yf thou bee a Subiecte thou muſte remember, and conſyder howe that powers be ordayned of God for the, yf thou be euyll to make the good by dewe correccyon: yf thou be good to make the[e] better, by the encoragemente of commendacyon, prayſe, and mayntenaunce. Looke therefore all you that haue power, and authorytye of GOD, that ye vſe it, as ye are commaunded by God: to correcte and punyſhe the euyll doer, and to encorage, rewarde, and mayntaine the good.

Se that for ſo ferre as your power extendeth, there be no euyll vnpunyſhed, nor no good vnrewarded. But harcke a lytle, and I ſhal tell you of an ab[h]omynable robbery done in the Citye, knowen to the officers of the city, and as yet not punyſhed, but rather mayntayned in the city. There is a greate ſumme of monye ſente from an honorable Lord by hys ſeruaunte vnto thoſe whome he is indetted vnto in the citye. The officers knowynge that they to whom thys monye is ſente haue great nede of it, knowe alſo in what places, at what tymes theſe vnthryſtye ſeruauntes by whome it is ſente, at gamnynge, banckettyng, and riot, do ſpende it. If thys be an euell dede, why is it not punyſhed? Bycauſe it is not knowen ſome ſaye. But whyther they meane that it is not knowen to be done, or not knowen to be euyll I doubte. And therefore here now wyll I make it openlye knowen boeth to be done, and alſo to be euell done, and worſe ſuffered. But doeth not manye of you knowe? ſure I am that all you that be officers oughte to know that all that ryches and treaſures whyche rych men, and rufflers, waſte at gredye gamning, glotonous banketting, and ſuche riote, is not theyr owne, but ſente by theym from the honorable Lord of heauen, vnto other that be honeſt, pore,

[1] 1 Peter *ii*. 14.

and nedye: vnto whome God by hys promyſe is indetted. Ye knowe, that *Domini eſt terra et plenitudo
eius.*[1] The yearthe is the Lordes, and the plenty
therof. So that no man hath any thyng of hys owne:
But hath receyued all of the Lorde. For, *Quid habes
quod non accepiſti?*[2] What haſte thou that thou haſt
not receyued: Yea thou as a ſeruaunte haſte receyued of thy Lord, whych gyueth vnto hys ſeruauntes the Talentes of hys treaſures. And to knowe
for what purpoſe he gyueth theym vnto you, reade
Eſaye, the xviii [.lviij.]. *Frange eſurienti panem tuum. etc.*[3]
Breacke thy breade vnto the hungrye, and the nedye:
and the wanderyng leade into thy houſe: whan thou
ſeeſt one naked cloth hym, and do not dyſpyſe thyne
owne fleſhe. Heare you ſeruauntes of the Lorde,
whyche haue receyued the treaſures of the lord, vnto
whom the lorde by you hath ſente them: vnto the
houngrye, the nedye, the naked, and thoſe that be of
the ſame fleſhe and bloude that you youre ſelues be.
Nowe you offycers knowynge that greate ryches, and
treaſures ſente from the honorable lord of heauen,
vnto his welbeloued people, the nedy members of
Chriſtes bodye, by theſe vnthriſtye ſeruauntes is ſpente
at gamnynge, and riote, within your offyces, ye muſte
nedes knowe that an euyll dede is done. Let vs
therfore I praye you, knowe howe it is punyſhed.
Peraduenture ye wyll ſaye: ther is no lawe in England that appoynteth any punyſhmente for gamners.
If therefore euyll dedes maye be done in Englande
wythout feare, than is the ſweard of authoritye borne
in Englande, wythout a cauſe. But I wyll tell the
that art an offycer in England or in what Chryſten
lande ſo euer it be: whereas there is no certayne
punyſhment for any euyl dede by mans law, there the
offycer may and ought to vſe any kind of puniſhment
to amende or reſtreyne the euyll doer, by goddes
lawe. But without doubte yf thoſe ſame men ſhould
ſpende in the ſame ſorte of ryot, ſo great treaſures
ſente from the Kynges Maieſtye vnto the Aldermenne

---

[1] Psa. *xxiv.* 1.   [2] 1 Cor. *iv.* 7.   [3] Isa. *lviii.* 7.

of thys Cytye, there fhoulde be punyfhmente, correccyon, and reamedye founde for theym quyckely.

And of very confcience is not god as much to be feared as the kynge, and the poore, and nedye as well to be pytied and prouyded for as the rych and wealthy?

Well, gamners, ryotters, and all euell doers, yf they do not repente, fhalbe damned in theyr owne fynnes: but the bloude of theyr foules fhalbe requyred at the handes of the offycers, whyche by feare fhoulde haue caufed theim to leaue fynne. Yea but what fhall me [we] than faye by vfurye, whyche is nowe made fo lawefull that an offycer yf he would, can not punyfh, to make men to leaue it? As concernynge thys matter we haue playne commaundemente in the fiftene of Deutro[nomie]. And in the fyfte of Math. To lend to hym that nedeth, and wold borowe. And in the fyxte of Luke it is playne. *Date mutuo, nihil inde fperantes.*[1] Lende fayeth Chrifte, trufting to haue no gayn therby. Here we haue two commaundementes, the one is to lende, and the other not to lende for lukar [lucre]: nowe he that breaketh goddes commaundement muft nedes go to the deuyll. So that in breakynge thefe two commaundementes, here is two wayes for you ryche men to go to the dyuyll: Eyther in lendynge for luker [lucre], or els in not lendynge anye thynge at all. Manye of you there be, that whofoeuer fayeth nay, wyll nedes the one of thefe two wayes. For yf mans lawe do ftop vp vfurye, fo yat by lendyng thou canft haue no gaynes, than wylte thou the other waye apace, and lend nothyng at all. So fhalte thou be fuer to come ther away to the deuyll. For than fhall no man in no cafe haue anye vfe of thy goods. Therefore neyther the lawe, nor the officer in fufferynge a lytle vfurye, and commaundinge none, doth mayntayne or allow vfurye. But for becaufe you [thou] beynge an vfurer wylte nedes to the dyuell, they fuffer the to goo fuch awaye as fome commodytye myght come to other by fome vfe of thy goodes, rather than by ftoppynge vp that

[1] Luke *vi.* 35.

waye, to dryue the there awaye as no man coulde haue any vfe of anye of thy goodes. For where as God commaundeth, and thy nedy neyghbour defyreth the to lende, and thou neyther at the reuerence of God, nor for pitye of thy neyghboure wylte lende of loue frelye: but contrarye to goddes commaundemente wyth out pytye of the poore, thou wylte not ftycke to lende for gredyneffe of luker couetouflye: thy owne dedes declare the to be fo voyde of all godly charity, and fo ful of diuilyfh couetoufnes, that thou art fer paft all mans cure, and helpe, either by law or punifhmente. So wyl I leue the, and fpeake of thofe that myght, and oughte to be healed by men beynge in authorytye, and yet wyll not.

For ther be fum fuche ioyly felowes that they wylbe fubiect to no powers, which by fear myght caufe them to forbeare theyr vayne pleafures in euil: vnto thofe now confequentlye doth [faincte] Paule fpeake, fayinge: ye muft nedes be fubiecte, not onely for wrathe, but alfo for confcience fake. If ye be fuche ioyly felowes that ye feare not the wrathe or dyfpleafure of officers, whan as ye do euyll, yet grope youre owne confcience, that ye may fele what a greuous fynne it is to wythftande the powers ordayned of GOD to minifter dewe correccyon vnto euyll doers. For not onely thy confcyence, but alfo thyne owne deede in that thou doefte paye tribute for thys thynge, fhall teftifye agaynft the: that thou knoweft theym to be the myniflers of GOD, attendynge to thys fame thynge, to thys bryngynge euell doers in feare. It is therefore a matter of confcience for the[e] fo to withftande the powers ordayned of God, that thei take no place in the, but that thou wylt do euell wythout feare, and maintaine that whych is euell done, by worfe prefumpcion. I do not faye that whatfoeuer the magyftrates commaunde is a matter of confcience, but what foeuer is euell, is a matter of confcyence. And to refyfte ryghte by myghte, fo that thou wylte not be fubiecte in humylitye, vnto thofe powers whyche God by hys righte hath fet ouer the[e] in authoritye is a greate euell, and therefore a greate matter of confcience. Manye examples we haue whyche doeth proue that euerye commaundement of magiftrates be not matters in confcience, and yet euery refifting or rebelling againft their autority is a matter in confcience. The Iewes had a cuftume confirmed by their elders whiche were magiftrates, that no man fhould eate wyth vnwafhen handes: Chrifte Iefu leafte thys cuftome, brake thys tradicion wythout any grudge of confcience.

Dauid knowynge Saule the kyng to be a wycked man and hys deadly enemy, and hauyng Saule in a denne, where as if he would, he myghte haue kylled hym: this Dauid hadde a good confcience not to touche the lordes anointed, to fuffer Saule to be kynge and to fubmitte hym felfe. Daniel was commaunded not to praye to God: the Apoftles were commaunded not to preache gods worde. Thefe dyd not rebell againft the higher powers, no nor yet for confcience obey men, but rather they obeyed God. For Daniell did praye, and the Apoftles dyd preache. So ryfe not, rebell not, refifte not, what foeuer the rulers them felues do: And be ye not fo fcrupulous as to thynke the bond in confcience vnto euerye thing that a man beyng a ruler commaundeth the to do it efpeciallye, if God commaund the contrary. Nowe it foloweth, geue vnto euerye one that which is due: Euery dutye belonging to euery body, can not here be declared, no nor at this tyme rehearfed, I wyll therefore fpeake briefely of one thynge whych fhall be a generall example for all duties. Pau. i. vnto the Cor. xi. *Vnus panis vnum corpus multi fumus :*[1] One bred fayeth he one body we are that be many: by the whiche he declareth that as of diuers cornes of wheate by the liquor of water knoden into dough is made one loafe of breade: fo we being diuerfe men, by loue and charitie, whyche is the liquor of lyfe, ioyned into one congregacion, be made as dyuers members of one mifticall body of Chrifte, where by I

---

[1] 1 Cor. x. 17.

say, as by one example in the ſtede of many, learne that the more gorgeous you youre ſelues bee in ſilkesand veluettes, the more ſhame is it for you to ſee other poore and neady, beyng members of the ſame bodye, in ragges and clothe, yea bare and naked.

Doeſt thou not thynke them to be members of the ſame bodye that thou arte? Then arte not thou a member of Chriſte, then arte not thou a chylde of God, then art not thou a chriſten man. One member oughte as well to be prouided for, as a nother: I do not ſay that one oughte to haue as coſtely prouiſion as a nother.

But as there be dyuers members in dyuers places, hauyng dyuers duties, ſo to haue dyuers prouiſion in feedyng and clothyng.

And as they be all in one body, ſo none to be without that feedynge and clothyng, whych for that part of the bodye is meete and neceſſarye. Euen as ye do prouide indifferentlye for euery parte of youre naturall bodye, by reaſon of the which, ye are bounde, and ſubiecte to corruption: So let no parte or member of your Chriſten bodye be vnprouyded for: By reaſon of the whyche bodye, ye be heyres of the heauenly kyngdome. And this one example generally ſhall teache you to gyue that whych is due vnto euery one ſeuerally. Nowe here foloweth euen. iiii. [fower] wordes: Tribute, cuſtume, fere, honor. Of theſe. iiii. [fower] wordes wil I conclude almoſt in iiii. [fower] wordes. Ye muſt gyue trybute, to whome trybute is due: cuſtome, to whome cuſtome is due: feare, to whome feare is due: honour, to whome honoure is due. Vnder trybute be conteined taxes, fiftenth, ſubſides, and ſuche as be payed at ſometymes to the Rulers, and be not continuall. Cuſtomes be tythes, tolles, rentes, and ſuch as the people paye vnto the officers continually. For payinge of trybute beſydes thys commaundemente of Paule, we haue example of Chriſtes mother, whych beyng at the houre of her trauell went out of Galyle vnto Bethlem, a toune in Iewry, there to be taxed, and pay trybute vnto Cefar.

As concernyng cuſtome, Chriſt hymfelfe commaunded Peter to pay for them both, leſt that they ſhulde offend: that is, leſt that they, in not paying, ſhuld geue euyll example vnto the people. So Chriſten men muſt nedes paye both trybute and cuſtome. What trybute and cuſtome good men may take, it appereth in that that goeth afore: furelye euen fo muche and no more as ſhall fufficientlye difcharge their coſtes, neceſſaryly beſtowed in correctynge of euyll, and rewardyng good. Marke that I fay they may or oughte to take no more: for here I tell them their duty. For truly if they do requyre more of you that be their fubiectes, then is it youre duty to pay that whiche they aſke, and not to be curyous to know for what caufe it is aſked, but this onlye to take hede that with due reuerence ye pay it, as Paule commaundeth, and as Chriſte and hys mother haue geuen you example. Feare and honoure belonge chieflye, yea in a manner onely vnto God. For God onely for hym felfe is to be feared and honoured.

All other for gods caufe, are fo to be feared and honoured: as that feare and honoure which is geuen vnto them, may procede and come finally vnto God. For, *dominum deum tuum adorabis et illum folum coles.*[1] Thou ſhalte honoure the Lorde thy God, and hym only ſhalt thou reuerentlye ferue. As for the Deuyll, feare hym not, for he wyll doo no leſſe harme vnto thee then he canne: he canne do no more then God wyll fuffer hym. Feare therfore leſte that thou offende God, and he fufferre the Deuyll to vtter hys malyce, and myfchyefe towardes thee.

That feare, honoure, or feruice whyche accordynge to goddes commaundemente is done vnto thofe perfonnes whom God hath authoryfed to receyue it in hys name, is done vnto God.

As that money whych by thy commaundemente is payde to thy feruaunt in thy name, is paid vnto the[e].

[1] Matt. *iv.* 10.

Therefore Chrifte rulynge in magiftrates by authorytye, and beynge houngrye and coulde in the poore by pytye, doeth commaunde vs to geue, and promyfeth that he hym felfe wyll receyue and rewarde that honoure of reuerence, feruyce and obedyence doone to the hygher powers, as to hys ordinaunce in the common wealth: and alfo that honour of charitable almes [almose], relyefe, and conforte, whych is beftowed vpon the poore and neady, as vpon the lyuely members of his owne body. As for that whych wythout goddes commaundement, of mans phantafticall imaginacion is doone vnto Images, muft nedes be hyghe dyfhonoure, and greuous difpleafure vnto God, when as the lyuely ymage of God created wyth hys owne hande in flefhe and bloud, doth honor, reuerence, and homage vnto a dead picture of man, grauen in ftocke or ftone, wyth a workemans tooles.

God is alfo honoured in all hys creatures, when as they be taken wyth thankes, and vfed as he hath commaunded: and therfore, when as they be vnthankfully taken, or wyckedly abufed, then is he difhonoured, and difpleafed.

Nowe, heare a fhort conclufion, *Qui ex deo eft, uerbum dei audit*. He that is of God, heareth the worde of God. All you I faye that be Chriften men, Gods chyldren, and indued wyth Goddes fpiryte, wyll heare the worde of Gods threatenyng, and fearyng his vengeaunce, repent, wyll heare the woorde of gods commaundement, and folowyng his counfels amende youre lyues, wyl heare the worde of Gods promyfe, and paciently fufferynge, truft to hys goodnes. As for you that wyll not heare and regarde goddes worde, ye declare your felues not to be of God. But for becaufe ye haue the deuyl to your father, ye wyll fulfyll the luftes and defyres of the Deuyll, whyche is your father. And the lufte and defire of the Deuyll is, to hynder the worcke and pleafure of God: and thys is the worke and wyll of God, that we fhould repofe

oure faythe and trufte in Chrifte Iefu, and beftowe oure
laboure and diligence in our owne vocacyon.

Therefore the deuyll poyfonynge all hys wyth
greadye couetoufenes, wyll caufe them euer to truft
to their owne prouifion, and neuer to be content wyth
their owne vocacion, but beynge called of God to be
marchaunt, gentleman, lawer, or courtear, yet to be
readye at a becke of their father the deuyl, befydes
this their godly vocacion, deuyllyfhelye to proule for,
feke, and purchafe farmes, perfonages, and benefices,
to difcourage houfbandemenne from tyllynge of the
grounde, and minifters from preachynge of Goddes
woorde: that therby maye come a greuoufe honger,
dearth, and lacke both of naturall fubftaunce for the
bodye, and alfo of heauenly foode for the foule And
then thofe in the countrey that be not gods chyldren,
but deuyllyfhe vipers, will hyffe, whifper, and fwell
wyth venemous prefumpcion, and their fting of rebellion to deftroy both them felues, and al the cuntry.
But they of ye cuntry or els wher, that be the chyldren
of God in dede, knowynge couetous riche men and
officers to be fparpled abrod in the cuntry as the
fcourges of god, to beat them for their fynnes, lyke
gentle chyldren, wyl acknowledge their owne fautes,
and paciently fuffryng correccion, pitifullye crye vnto
their heauenly father for mercy, forgeueneffe, and conforte. So all you in England, that haue any godly
knowledge, grace, and charitie, wyll fay with the prophet Dauid: *Virga tua, et baculus tuus, ipfa me con-
folata funt*:[1] Thy rod, O Lorde and thy ftaffe, they it
be whyche haue conforted me. Thy rodde of correccion, whych is thefe couetous ryche men, and officers,
and thy ftaffe of conforte, whyche is the kynges maieftie, whom thou haft endowed wyth a gracious gentle
nature, godly educacion, wonderful wyt, and great
learnyng: yea, and thofe noble men whom thou haft
called from their vayne plefures, to take great paynes,
of a reuerent loue towardes the kyng, and of a chari-

[1] Ps. xxiii. 4.

in the Shroudes in Poules. 51

table pitie towardes vs, to beftowe their landes and goodes, tyme, and ftudye, and all that euer they haue, to profper the Kynge, to prouide for hys realme, and to cherifh vs his people therof. Thus thy rodde of correccion, O Lorde, hath taught vs to be fubiecte in humilitie vnto all hygher powers, as to thy ordinaunce: and this thy ftaffe of conforte o Lorde, doth encorage vs to loue and truft them, efpecially vnto whome thou haft geuen hyeft power and authoritie. So that we can nowe wyilynglye geue vnto euerye one that whyche is due: vnto ye higher powers, reuerence, feruyce, and obedience, vnto all in general faythfull dealynge, and vnto the poore and needye, charitable almes [almofe], releefe and conforte.

Giue therfore vnto vs, o Lord, mercye and grace, that we maye render vnto thee thankes and prayfe for euer. Amen.

¶ Imprinted at London by John Daie, dwellinge ouer Aldersgate, and Wylliam Seres dwelling in Peter Colledge.
The yeare of our Lorde God M. D. L. the nynth daye of Aprill.

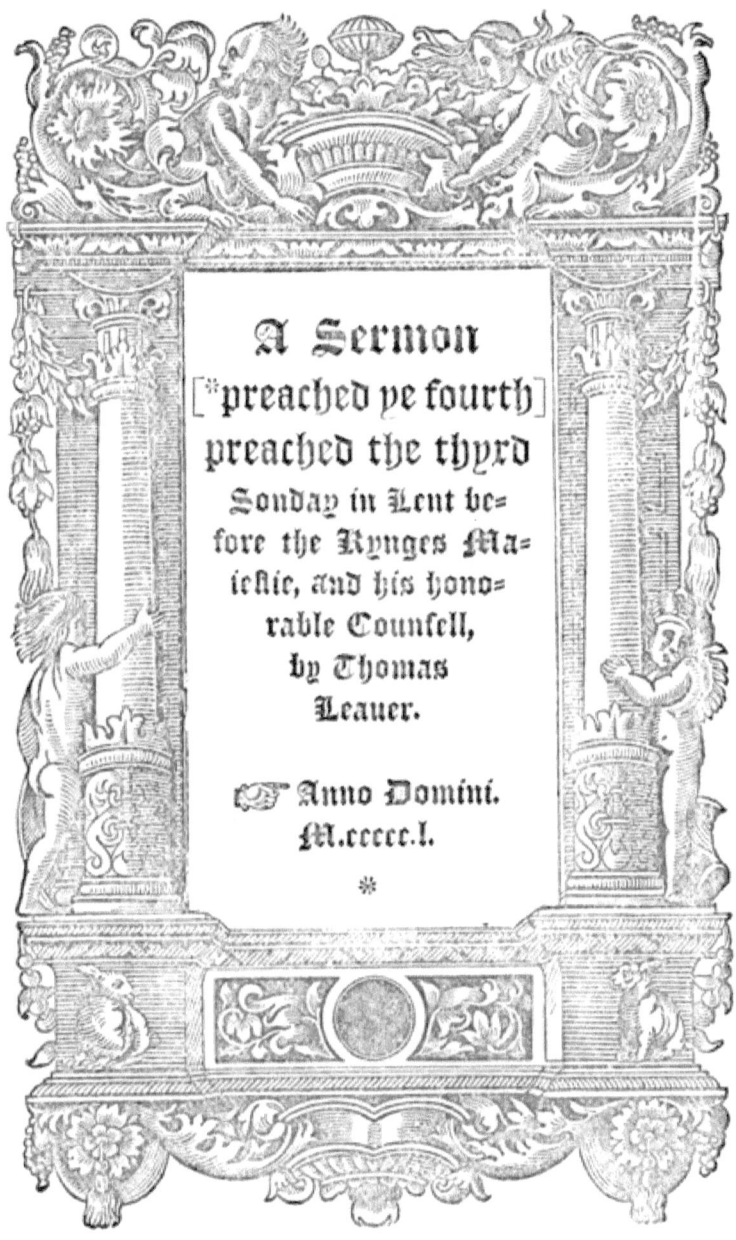

A Sermon
[*preached ye fourth]
preached the thyrd
Sonday in Lent be=
fore the Kynges Ma=
iestie, and his hono=
rable Counsell,
by Thomas
Leauer.

☞ Anno Domini.
M.ccccc.l.

☞ *Cum priuilegio imprimendum solum.*

* As incorrectly printed on some title pages to this sermon.

In nomine Iesu Christi.

OD be mercifull vnto vs: For the tyme is euen nowe comynge, when as God muste needes either of his mercye here in Englande, worke suche a wonderfull miracle vnto our conforte, as farre passeth mans expectacion: orels of his righteousnes take such vengeance of this lande to th[e]example of all other landes, as shall be to our vtter distruccion.

Ye know, that immediatly after the preachynge of Noe, came the great floud that drouned ye world. After the warnyng of Loth, came fyre, brymstone vpon the Sodomites and Gomorrians. When Moises had declared Gods thretnynges in Egipte, kyng Pharao and his people were plaged vpon the lande, and drouned in the red sea.

Suche plages came euer where Gods worde truly preached, is not beleued, receaued, and folowed. But at the preachyng of Ionas, the Niniuites repented wonderfully. When the boke of the law was reade vnto Iosias the kyng, he, with all his people spedely repentyng, found exceadyng mercy, blessyng, and grace: as lykewyse all other shalbe sure to find, which heare the worde of God and keepe it.

For when Christ and his Apostles had preached the Gospel vnto the Iewes, those that beleued were delyuered frome the curse of the law, vnto the blessing of grace, out of worldly misery, to be inheriters of the heuenly kyngdome: and those that did not beleue, were cast from God, oppressed of men, ouercome, spoyled, murthered, and distroyed of their enemyes.

Wherfore Englande, whiche at this present tyme, by

reason of the worde of God setfurth, reade, preached, and comuned, dothe in euerye place heare the counsell of Noe, the warnynge of Loth, the law of Moyses, the threatnynges of the Prophetes, and the grace of the Gospell, as it was declared and taught by Christ and his Apostles: Thys Englande muste nedes, either by beleuynge of these thynges, obteyne of God wonderfull grace of amendement, orels by neglecting them, prouoke the vengeance of God, as a dewe plage and punyshment.

Take heede therfore England, for if thou by vnbelefe, let and stop God from workynge of miracles to thy confort, then surely dooest thou prouoke God to powre doun vengeaunce vpon the, to thy vtter distruccion: But if thou doo regarde, receaue, and beleue Gods worde, he wyll worke wonderfull miracles to thy conforte, wealthe, and prosperitie. Yea, let euerye man, of what estate or degree soeuer he be, grope his owne conscience: for if he dooe not there feele that the worde of God dothe take place to moue hym to repentaunce and amendment of lyfe, then shall he be sure sone to haue experience, that the vengeaunce of God, by a shamefull shorte ende of his wretched lyfe, wyll bryng him vnto an euerlastynge dampnable deathe. For all those that wyll not creepe vnder the merciful wings of god, as the chikynnes of Christ, shalbe caught and deuoured of puttockes, haukes, and kytes, as a pray for the deuyll. The wynges of God be stretched abrode here in Englande, by the kynges gracious maiestye and his honorable counsell, of mighty power, with ready wyll to shadowe, defende, and saue all those that with reuerent loue, come humbly creepyng vnder their ordinaunce, rule, and gouernaunce, whiche is the power, the wynges, and the honour [the order] of God.

The filthye gredye puttockes, wylde haukes, and rauenyng kytes be supersticious papistes, carnall gospellers, and sedicious rebelles, which as ye haue seene, by late experience, haue most cruelly caught, spoyled, and

deuoured the lambes, the chekynnes, the chyldren of
God, redemed and boughte with Chriftes bloude.
Wherfore as Chrift in his owne perfone dyd once
lament and bewayle Ierufalem, fo dothe he nowe
many tymes in the perfons of his propheticall Preachers,
lament and bewayl Englande, faying: O England,
howe ofte wolde I haue gathered thy chyldren, as a
hen gathereth her chikens vnder her wynges, and thou
woldeft not. Euen with the fame affeccion that the
fhepherde cryeth, feeyng the wolfe le[e]ryng towardes the
fhepe, and with the fame affeccion that the hen clock-
eth and calleth, fpyeng the kyte houeryng ouer her
chekyns: with the fame affeccion it behoueth the
minifter and preacher of God, feeyng vntollerable
vengeaunce hangynge ouer Englande, to crye, to call,
and to geue warnyng vnto the people, faying as [it] is
written in the firft of Efay: If ye willyngly wyl heare
and obeye, ye fhall eate the good confortable frutes
of the earthe: but if ye wyll not, and prouoke me
vnto angre, the fwoorde fhall deuoure you: *Quia os
Domini locutum eft.*[1] For it is the mouth of the lord
that hath fpoken.

Now your reuerende maieftie, moft gracious kyng,
and you honourable wyfe godly counfellers, you are
the chiefe fhepherdes, you are the moft reuerende
fathers in Chrifte, hauynge the wynges of power and
authoritie, to fhadow, faue, and keepe thefe lambes of
god, thefe [the] chekens of Chrift, and thefe chyldren of
the heauenly father, redemed with Chriftes bloude,
and committed vnto your handes, to be faued, kepte,
and prouyded for.

God be prayfed, with thankful obedience, and louynge reuerence dewe to your gracious maieftye and
honorable counfell, whiche haue furely wyfely prouyded for, diligently kept, and charitably faued this
realme, by driuyng away the wylde [wilie] foxe of
papifticall fuperfticion, and by caftynge out the vncleane fpirit of ignorance, to gods glorye, your honour,
and our confort.

[1] Is. *i.* 20.

But alas moſt gracious Kyng and godly gouernors, for the tender mercyes of God, in our Sauiour Ieſu Chriſt, take good and diligent heede when ye be chaſyng the wylde [wilie] fox of papiſticall ſuperſticion, that the greedye wolfe of couetous ambicion, do not creepe in at your backes: For ſurely he wyll doo more harme in a weeke, then the foxe dyd in a yere.

Take heede, that the vncleane ſpirite of ignoraunce, returnynge with. vii. other worſe then himſelf, fynde no place vnwarded, where he may creepe in agayne. For if he returnyng with his felowes, enter in agayne, then wyll he make the ende of this generacion to bee worſe then the begynnyng.

Then ſhall you leeſe the rewarde of your former diligence, and be dam[p]ned for your later negligence. Then ſhall the welſpryng of mercye, which of long tyme hath watered thys Realme with the grace of God be cloſed vp, and the blodye floudes of vengeance guſhing out from the wrath and indignacion of God, ouerflowe all togyther. Then wyll not God, by workyng of miracles declare mercy, but by takynge of vengeaunce, execute rightouſnes.

But God beyng as mercyfull yet, as euer he was, if you contynewe as faythfull, wyſe, and dilygent as ye haue ben, to handle the wolfe, as you haue doone the foxe, to keepe out the deuyll, as to caſt out the deuyll: then ſhall the people of this lande feede in quyetnes, without feare of euyl: then ſhal you continuyng to the[e]nde, be ſure of an hunderdfold reward in this lyfe, and afterwards, euerlaſting lyfe, ioye and glorye. Then ſhall God doo wonderfull miracles in Englande, to declare howe mercy ſhall triumphe ouer rightouſnes.

And that wee maye all dyſpoſe our ſelfes the more conuenientlye for God to worke ſuche a miracle amonge vs, wee haue appoynted for the goſpell of this day, writen in the. vi. of Iohan, a wonderfull miracle of. v. thouſande men, fed and ſatisfyed with. v. loaues and ii. fyſhes, wheras euery man may and ought to learne his owne dutye, whiche ſhall cleare[ly] appeare too a kyng in Chriſt, to head gouerners vnder the kynge, in the Apoſtles, beyng moſt neare about Chriſt, and to all other men, in that multitude of the people, whiche folowynge Chriſt, were obedient to ſyt doune at the commaundment of his Diſciples, not knowyng, nor enquiring why they were ſo commaunded.

And as ſurely as this wonderfull miracle was done to the great confort of them in Chriſtes tyme: ſo truly is it left in writyng for to learne vs by pacience and confort of the Scriptures, to haue good hope at this tyme.

And as Chriſte, hauynge alwayes ſpeciall reſpecte vnto hys audience, dyd teache the fyſhers by talkyng of nettes, preachynge vnto the Iewes by dyuers parables, and called the Gentyles by the eloquence of Paule: ſo I, in handlyng of this miracle, hauing reſpect vnto thys audience, wyll applye the wonderfull great charitable prouiſion of Chriſte, vnto the Kynges Maieſtye: the faythfull diligence of the Apoſtles, vnto the nobilitie: and the dewe obedience and hertye thankfulnes of the multitude, vnto all other of the communaltye. Not doubtyng but that charitable prouiſion of liberall benefites, wyll be a thyng moſt pleſaunt and honorable for the Kynges Gracious Maieſtye, and faythfull diligence in diſpoſyng great benefites moſt conuenient, and commendable for all that be in high authoritie: and finally, humble obedience, and vnſayned thankfulnes to be moſt neceſſary, requiſite, and looked for at this tyme, in all inferiours and commune ſorte of people in Englande.

Marke a litle after the begynnyng of the ſyxt Chap. of Iohan, and ye ſhall heare, when as much people [commyng vnto Ieſus, hauyng nothyng to] eate, what Ieſus dyd. I wyll paſſe the diſcripcion of the wyldernes, with the cauſes and the maner of the peoples goyng togither, and begynne at that whiche Chriſt dyd, when they were cummyng towardes hym.

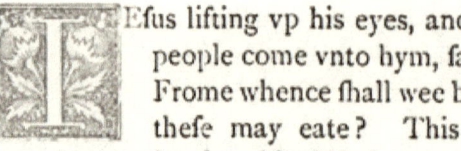Efus lifting vp his eyes, and feeynge muche people come vnto hym, fayde vnto Philip: Frome whence fhall wee b[u]ye bread, that thefe may eate? This he fayd temptyng hym: for he himfelf knew what he wolde do. Philippe anfwered vnto hym: Two hundreth penye worth of breade wyll not be fufficient vnto thefe fo that euerye one myght take a lytell. One of hys difciples Andrew, Symon Peters brother, fayth vnto hym: There is one boye here, whych hath .v. barley loaues and .ii. fyfhes, but what ar thofe amongeft fo many? Iefus faid: Make the men to fyt doun. There was muche graffe in the place. The men therefore fat doune, about the numbre of .v. thoufands. Iefus tooke the breade, and after thankes geuynge, dyd diuide it vnto his difciples, and the difciples to them that were fette: And lykewyfe of the fyfhes, fo muche as they woulde. And when they were filled, he fayde vnto his difciples: Gather vp the broken meates remaynyng, that nothynge bee loft. They gathered therfore, and fylled .xii. bafkets full of thofe meats which remayned, after that thei hadde eaten. The men therfore feeynge what a fygne Iefus hadde done, fayde that this is trulye the Prophet whiche cummeth vnto the worlde.

O Mercifull Lorde, what a greef is it to fee thofe which a man loueth hertely, with fuche difeafes infected, that euery thing miniftred by the Phificion to doo them good, by their owne vnquietnes and mifufynge of the fame, doth encreafe their greuous daungerous fycknes. For thefe [people in the wilderneffe, deftitute of all prouifion, and in great lacke and neede of bodily fuftenaunce, were then by a wonderfull miracle, plentifully fedde of Chrift, occafionyng then by the yearthly and bodily foode, to defire and feeke the bread of life, defcendyng from heauen: but then tooke, and turned that occafion cleane contrary, imaginyng to make Chrifte an yearthly Kyng, and were fo greedie to feede their bodies, that thei had no defire nor taft of the foode of the foule. And now England hauyng occafion, by the abolifhyng of Papiftrie, to embrace fincere Chriftianitie, tourned that occafion, to take the fpoyle of Papiftrie, whiche is the caufe that many neglecte, and fclaunder fincere Chriftianitie. And fo haue, and doe tourne all occafions of godly charitable reformation, into worldly couetous corruption. And the] people [of this audience], hauyng great occafion of confort, bi reafon that in [t]his place, through the true preachyng of gods word, all fynne is plainly and freely rebuked: and thofe fynnes efpeciallye which dooe appertayne vnto magiftrates, wherby any man of indifferent iudgement, may thynke that thefe magiftrates beeyng prefent, and willingly hearynge, bee purpofed to amende: Thefe people I faye, that thus haue a great occafion of conforte offered vnto them, by their owne miftakyng of it, dooe tourne all to their further griefe and daunger. For they fpeake vnreuerently, and vntruly flaunder the magiftrats, not only with the faultes that bee here named, but alfo with rebukyng, imprifonyng, and forbiddyng of the Preachers. And when as by the fame mouth of the true preacher, their venemous tongues be rebuked, then thei fpare not to fay, that the Preacher hath learned his leffon in Iacke an apes court: doyng as much as lieth in them, to make other men, neither to reuerence the magiftrates, nor beleue the Preacher. What thei them felfes mean therebye, peraduenture by reafon of blyndneffe, they wot not. But we knowyng the craft of the deuyl, as Paul writeth. ii. Cor. ii. perceiue yat he wold haue nothing in this place layde to the Rulers charge: Not fearyng how muche be fpoken to thofe of the people, which be paft any amendment by wordes: But all that the deuyll feareth, is, left that the Rulers be put in remembraunce of the great daunger that they be in, for fufferynge fo great enormityes vnpunyfhed amongeft the people.

I therfore truftyng to do moft good in that whiche the deuyll laboureth the moft to hyndre, wyll laye great and many fautes vnto them that haue moft power and authoritie. For fure I am, that rulers ordeyned by God to fee the ignoraunt inftructed, and the euyll punyfhed, be in great daunger of Gods vengeaunce, for the great and manifolde enormities whiche do grow and fpring of ignoraunce, for lacke of knowledge, and of diffolutenes for lacke of due correccion.

And you people be ye fure that the more their daunger is, for lacke of prouifion and punyfhment for other mens faultes, the greater is the damnacion of them that commit and doo thefe fautes.

Nowe I truftyng to God, and not fearyng the deuyll, wyll proceede to declare and applye this parte of fcripture vnto this Audience, fo that for no man I wyll cloke or flatter anye vyce.

Iefus lyftyng vp his eyes, and feeynge muche people cummynge vnto hym, &c.

Here note two thynges: in the people note coming vnto Chrift, and in Chrift, note charitable prouifion for the people. For in this people dothe Chrift declare by example, and proue in experience his doctrine to be true, whiche he had afore taught, faying: Fyrft feeke for the kyngdome of God and the rightoufnes, therof, and all thefe other, meanyng neceffaryes, fhal bee miniftred vnto you. For here they folowyng Chrift, to feke the kyngdome of God, had not onlye this kingdome of God, this bread of lyfe, this woorde of faluacion preached vnto them, but alfo, all their difeafes healed, and their hungrye belyes withe good meates plentifully fylled.

Yea, the plentye of thefe people hauyng enough,

euen fo much as they woulde, was farre more then the plenty of crafty Lawers, difceitful Merchauntes, couetous greedyguttes, and ambicious prollers, whiche canne neuer haue ynough : but alwayes contynew in vnfaciable hunger, and neede of couetoufnes. As [in] the. [xx]xiiii. Pfal. declareth : *Diuites eguerunt*:[1] The ryche haue felt neede and hunger : but they whiche feeke the Lorde, lacke no goodneffe [gooddes].

He that feeketh to be ryche, be he neuer fo poore a flaue, or fo mightye a Lorde, he falleth into dyuers temptacions and fnares of the deuyll : but they that feeke the Lorde, fhall lacke no goodnes. Seke for to be ryche, and thou fhalt fynd forow, miferye, and mifcheif : Seeke for to be godlye, and thou fhalt fynd confort, welth and profperitie, with al maner of felicitie. If thou wylt be godly, thou muft folowe Chrift : thou muft not folow the fteppes of his feete, which be taken vp into heauen oute of thy fyght, but thou oughteft to folowe the doctrine of his worde, which is lefte here [here left] vpon earth, to guyde the fteppes of thy lyfe, in the way of peace. And whyther wyll Gods worde guide the in the tyme of thy trouble and neceffitie? Surely vnto the Lorde, whyche fayth: *Propter miferiam inopum*, *&c.*[2] For the miferyes fakes of the confortleffe, and fyghynges of the poore, now wyll I ryfe, fayth the Lorde.

O Lorde, feeynge thou hafte manye people in Englande, that as yet be in miferies without confort, and in pouertie, and lacke helpe, how dooeft thou aryfe vnto them? Vnto this the Lorde anfwereth, in the. xxxiiii. of Ezechiel: *Sufcitabo fuper eos paftorem vnum*,[3] *&c.* I wyll fet vp ouer theim one paftor, euen my feruaunt Dauid, he fhall feede theym, and he fhall be their paftor, and I the Lord, wyl be their God. This prophecye was written longe after Dauids tyme. Wherfore by Dauid here named, is fignified and meante fuche a Kyng as fhalbe as faythfull and diligent to keepe, feede, and cheryfh his fubiectes within hys owne Realme, as was Dauid to his people within Ifraell [, that fame is Chrift in his Kyngdome, in his aucthoritie?]

[1] Psa. *xxxiv.* 10 (Latin). [2] Psa. *xii.* 5. [3] Ezek. *xxiv.* 23.

[And] We hope trufte and beleue, that oure gracious Kyng, indued with the faythfull diligence of Dauid, is ordeyned of God, to gouerne, cherifh and feede vs the people of this his Realme. Wherfore accordynge to the[e]xample of Chrifte Iefu, moft Chriften and Gracious Kyng, for the reuerence of God, which hath fet you vpon the high hyll of honor and authoritie, lyft vp your gracious eyes of charitable pitie, and behold much people throughoute all Englande, comyng to feeke releefe, eafe, and conforte, fente from God vnto them, by your excellent Maieftye. For althoughe there hathe ben to much mercy fhewed vpon the generacion of vypers, the vngracious rebels: Yet is there manye poore people, whiche lyke fymple fheepe, fhorne to the bare fkynne, haue as yet little prouifion and great neede: euen as .v. thoufandes in wildernes folowed Chrift and his Apoftles, fo many thoufandes in Englande, paft all other hope and refuge, folow your gracious maieftye and honorable Counfell. For their perfons [parfones], which fhoulde lyke fhepheardes feede them, doo lyke thieues robbe, murther and fpoile them. And their landlords, which fhuld defend them, be moft heauye maifters vnto them: Yea, all maner of officers doo not their duties to kepe the people in good ordre, but rather take fuch fees as maketh the people veraye poore. Who fo hathe eyes, and wyll fee, mai eafely perceiue that thofe perfonages, which be moft in nombre, and greateft in value. Throughout all England be no fhepherds houfes to laye vp fodder to feede the poore fheepe of the parifh, but theeuyfh dennes, to conuey away great fpoyle from all the ryche men of the parifh. I fay ther is no perfon there to releeue the poore and nedy, with natural fuftinaunce in keepyng of houfe, and to feede all ingenerally with the heuenly foode of Gods woorde by preachynge: But there is a perfons deputie or fermer, which hauyng neither habilitie, power, nor aucthoritie to doo the perfons dutye in feedynge and teachyng the paryfh, is able, fufficient, and ftout ynough to chalenge and take for his mayfters dutie, the tenth parte of all the parifh. Likewife other officers take many fees, and do few dutyes: And efpecially landlordes take exceedynge fynes and rentes of theire tenauntes, and doo no good vnto their tenauntes.

Now my Lordes, bothe of the laitie and of the clergye, in the name of God, I aduertyfe you to take heede: for when the Lorde of all Lords fhal fee his flock fcatered, fpylte, and lofte, if he folowe the trace of the bloude, it wyll leade him euen ftreyght waye vnto this court, and vnto your houfes, where as thefe great theues which murther, fpoyle, and diftroye the flockes of Chrift, be receaued, kepte, and mainteyned.

For you mainteyne your chapleynes to take Pluralities, and your other feruauntes mo offyces then they can or wyll difcharge.

Fye for fynne and fhame, eyther gyue your feruauntes wages, or els let them go and ferue thofe which do gyue them wages. For nowe your chapleynes, your feruauntes, and you* your felues haue the perfons, the fhepherdes, and the offycers wages, and neither you nor they, nor no other dooeth the perfons, the fhepherdes or the ofiycers dutye, except peraduenture ye imagen that there is a paryfhe priefte, curate, whiche dooeth the perfons duty. But although ye do fo ymagen, yet the people do feele and perceyue that he doeth meane no other thing but pai your duty, paye your dutye. Yes forfoth, he miniftreth Gods facramentes, he fayeth his feruyce, and he readeth the homilies, as you fyne flatring cowrtiers, which fpeake by imaginacion, tearme it: But the rude lobbes of the countrey, whiche be to fymple to paynte a lye, fpeake foule and truly as they fynde it, and faye: He minifheth Gods facraments, he flubbers vp his feruice, and he can not reade the humbles. Yet is there fome that can reade very well: but how many of thofe be not either fuperfticious papyftes, orels carnall gofpellers, whiche by their euyll example of lyuyng, and worfe

E

doctrine, do farre more harme then they do good by their fayr reading and faiyng of feruyce. But put the cafe, as it maye be, that there bee at a benefyce in fome place at fomtime, fome good curate: all thofe fummes wyll make but a fewe in nombre, and yet ye fee many perfons in many places abfente from their benefices, whiche if they be feldome abfent, may be good, but if they be continually or for the moft part abfent, then can they be neither good, honeft nor godly. For if their duytie be vndone, then can no man excufe them: if it be doone, then is it by other, and not by them: and then why dooe they lyue of other mens labours? He that preacheth the gofpell, fhulde lyue vpon the gofpell, as God hath ordeyned: As for thofe, *Qui mollibus vefliuntur, in domibus Regum*,[1] whiche go gaye in Kynges houfes, and either mofell the labouring oxe, orels fpoyle the poore parifh in the countrey, be of the deuyls ordinaunce. As there is in all offyces, fome putte in by Chrift, fome by the deuyl: fo is there in perfonages [Parfonages], fome fente from Chrift as fhepherds to fede, and fome from the deuyll, as theues to deuoure. Yea, amongeft all kyndes of offycers, fome bee true Prophettes and fhepheardes in dede, and fome haue fhepe fkyns, and be rauenyng wolfes in deede. The one taketh paynes in doyng of his dutye, and the other feketh gaynes in profeffyng of his duty. Take heede of thofe, for they are erraunt theeues.

Alas, if all thofe whiche take the names and profeffyons of offycers, for defyre of luker and honor, and do not execute the duties belongynge to their offyces with paynful diligence, be errant theues, as they be in deede, then is there manye a ftronge erraunt theefe amongeft them that be called honeft, worfhipfull, and honorable men.

For they haue the names, the authorities and vauntages of thofe offyces giuen and payed vnto them, the dutyes of the whiche be veray flenderly or nothynge at al executed amongeft the people.

[1] Matt. xi. 8.

If I were in anye other place in all Englande, I could and wolde vfe an other trade of preachynge afore an other audience: but beyng called of God by your appoyntement vnto this place at this tyme, my confcience doth compell me to vfe this trade and no other, afore this folemne audience. Wherfore with dreede and feare of God, with charitable pitie of the people, with moft reuerende loue and homage vnto your honors, I muft needes crye with the prophet Efaie: *Principes Sodomæ, populus Gomorræ:*[1] Heare the woorde of the Lorde ye Princes of Sodome, ye people of Gomorra: *Quo mihi multitudo victimarum veftrarum:*[1] What care I for the great nombre of your facrifyces, *Dicit Dominus,* fayth the lord: rebukynge all the facrifices, ceremonies, and feaftes of the Iewes, which he himfelfe had commaunded to be obferued and kepte: by the which thyng left in writynge, he doth teache and commaunde me howe to fpeake of your wel doyng here in England. Heare therfore ye Princes of Sodome, and ye people of Gomor, thus fayth the Lord. What pleafure haue I, yea what care I for al your Englifhe Bibles, Homilies, and all youre other bookes: fet furthe no more godly feruyce to honor me with: I hate them all with my herte, they are greuous vnto me, I am wery of them: Yea, it is a great payne for me to fuffer them. Why, o lord, thefe be good, thefe be godly, and thefe be neceffary thynges.

Truth it is, the faulte is not in the thynges that be fet furthe, but in you that haue fet them furthe. *Manus enim veftræ plenæ funt fanguine:*[2] For your handes are ful of blood.

Your handes, your feruyces [feruice] and your houfes be ful of perfons lyuynges, Preachers liuynges, and offycers liuynges. And by you, the perfone hath his difpenfacion, the preacher is put to fcilence, and the offycer vnpunyfhed, for neclectynge of his dutye. And fo through the negligence of the kepers, [(]good order, which is the pale of the parke of this commune welth dekayed[)], the dere therof, moft dearly bought with

---

[1] Isa. *i.* 10, 11. [2] Isa. *i.* 15.

Chriftes bloude, haue ftrayed oute of theire owne feedynge, to diftroy the corne of all mens liuynges : Where as very neceffytie hath compelled you with fuch force to driue them backe, as muft needes diftroye manye of thofe dere. Thofe people I mean, which you haue cheryfhed and kept, and as yet doo loue and pitie aboue all other iewels, commodities and pleafures. Alas, thefe that take the liuynges, and doo not the dutyes of Perfons, Preachers, landlordes, Bailyes, and of other officers : Thefe flatterers, thefe wolfes in lambes fkyns, thefe deuyls in mens vyfers haue caufed you to be thought and taken as cruell oppreffers of thofe [thefe] people, whofe furious wylde rage ye dyd fuppreffe and keepe vnder, of veraye charitable pitie towardes them, and all other, whiche with that rebellious rage, fhulde haue be all togither diftroied, if the help of your power and aucthoritie had ben anye longer differed.

Surely, vntyll that thefe prollers for them felues, thefe children of the deuyll, thefe fowers of fedicion be taken out of the way, either by reformacion, or by diftruction, your charitable pitie and prouifion for the people, and their reuerende loue and obedience towardes you, fhall neuer be feene, felt, and knowen. Nowe, as Helye was gilty of the whordome, extorcion, and abhominacion of his fonnes, fo are your hertes full of crueltye, and your handes full of bloude, not fo muche by doyng, as by fufferyng all thefe euyls. Wherfore *Lauamini, mundi eftote* :[1] Wafh, and make your felfes cleane, with the teares of repentaunce. *Auferte malum cogitationum veftrarum ab oculis meis* :[1] Awai with the euil of your thoughtes from afore my eyes. Open your heartes, that the fworde of Gods word may come to wype awaye couitoufnes, whiche is the roote of all euyll, planted in your hertes. For if that roote continew there, than can no good fpring from you : but euen the moft pure and holfome woorde of God fette furth by you, continuyng in couitoufnes, wyll be abhominable in the fyght of God, offenfiue vnto

---

[1] Isa. *i.* 16.

the people, and damnable vnto your felues. Wherfore, *Quiefcite agere peruerfe* :[1] Seace to peruerte, manye thynges from euyll vnto worfe. *Difcite benefacere* :[1] Learne to do well, in conformyng al thyngs that be amiffe, vnto a good ordre. *Quærite iudicium* :[1] Seeke [Searche] for righteous iudgement, which is almoft banyfhed out of Englande. Alas what a iudgement is this, a fuperfticious papifte, whiche hathe made the faulte, fhall haue a penfion out of a Chauntrie, fo longe as he lyueth, and a poore paryfhe whiche hathe great neede and doone no faulte, fhall lofe and forfayte many Chauntries vtterly for euer. *Subuenite oppreffo* :[1] Helpe the oppreffed people that be loaden with heuye burdeyns of paiynge wages to manye offyces, and faynte for lacke of releefe, and due feruyce of the offycer. *Iudicate pupillo* :[1] Iudge fo to the fatherles chyldrens behofe, that wardfhip mai be a good prouifion for fatherles chyldren, and not an vncharitable fpoyle of yong mens landes. *Defendite viduam* :[1] Shielde the wydow from all mens iniuryes, and compell them not to marye your vnthrifty feruauntes.

Thus hath God by Efaye in his tyme, and by me at this tyme defcribed Rulers Faultes, with a waye how to amende them. Therfore, *Principes Angliæ* :[1] Ye head rulers and gouernors of England, fyrft fee, acknowledge and* amende your owne fautes: And then, perufynge all vnder offycers, confyder, and note how few fhepheards and offycers doo feede and keepe, by doyng dutyes, and how many theeues, and wolfes do robbe and fpoyle the flockes, by takyng fees here in Englande: and then fhall ye perceaue that there muft nedes be manye fheepe, that with their hertes, myndes, and expectacion, do folow the Kynges Maieftye, and you of his honorable counfell, fo farre pafte the houfes and cyties of their owne prouifion, that yf thei haue not fpedy reliefe at your handes, many of them is lyke to feynte and decaye by the way.

Therfore this confydered and knowen, as Chrift lyftyng vp his eyes, dyd teache you to fee and con-

[1] Isa. *i*. 16, 17.

fyder the people: fo learne by that whiche foloweth in Chriftes dooyng, what fhalbe your dutye after that ye fee and knowe the multitude, the ftate and condicion of the people.

And he fayd vnto Philip: From whence fhall we bye breade, that thefe maye eate? But this he fayde to proue him: for he him felfe knewe what he wolde doo.

Chrift faid to Philip, as euery Chriften King ought to fay to his Counfell: From whence fhal we that be gouernors, kepers and feders, bye and prouide with our own coftes, labor, and diligence, bread, foode and neceffaryes, that thefe may eate and be releued, which be our fubiectes, in obedience, brethern in Chrift, and felow heyres of the heauenly kyngdome.

Pharao with his Counfell in Egipte, confulted howe to bryng the welthy people vnto miferye: fo that he is a very Pharonicall tyrant, which laboreth by oppreffion to thruft down the welthy people: And he is a faythful chriften kyng, that humbleth himfelfe by diligence to releeue, conforte, and fet vp the afflycted people. For the one, by worldiy policy, wolde haue much honor, and the other of godlye charitie wyll do much good. Chrift alfo fayde this, to proue and trye Philip, knowyng him felfe what fhoulde be done. So that here, Kynges and great men may lerne to trye and proue the honeftye, wyt, and fidelitie of their Counfellers in fuch matters as they them felues be fo perfect that they can difcerne with what difcrecion and mynde the Counfeller doth anfwere.

[And in this we maie fe, that God doeth not lacke, or neede any counfaile, or helpe of any manne, to dooe any good thyng, but would haue men to vnderftande how muche and wel that God, and how little or nothing menne can deuife, and dooe when as neede is. So therefore will God vfe, and exercife men, as Chrift here doeth vfe, and exercife Phillip, Andrewe, and the other Difciples, for their owne neceffitie, comforte, and commoditie to receiue, and learne of hym, wherewith they maie dooe good vnto others. And this leſſon had not Phillip yet learned.]

Philip aunſwered, that two hundreth peny worth of breade wyll not ſerue vnto theſe, ſo that euerye one myght take a lytell.

In the which anſwere, as concernyng his wytte, he declareth it to be to ſlender to prouyde for ſo great a matter in ſo ſhort tyme. And his mynde ſeemed to be ſuch, as wolde not haue Chriſt to trouble him ſelfe with ſo great cares, but rather as the other Euangeliſtes do declare, to ſende the people awai, and let them prouide for them ſelfes. The ſame mynde and affection was in Peter, after that Chriſt hadde tolde his Diſciples howe that he muſt go to Ieruſalem to ſuffer ſore paynes and miſerable death. For then Peter tooke him a ſyde and ſayde: Maiſter, fauour your ſelfe, doo not entre in to ſuche daunger and ſorowes.

And it is not vnlyke, but if your Mageſtye, with your Counſell, ſpeake vnto your nobles for prouiſion now to be made for the people, ye ſhall fynde ſome that bee Philippians and Peters, whiche by ſettynge afore your eyes the hardnes of the matter, the tendernes of your yeares, and the wonderfull charges that ſhulde be requiſite, wyll moue and counſell you to quiet youre ſelfe, to take your eaſe, yea, to take your paſtyme, in haukyng, huntyng or gamnyng. Vnto whom your Mageſtie may anſwere, as Chriſte dyd vnto Peter: Auoide fro me Sathan, thou hyndreſt me by thy carnall temptacion, to doo that thynge whiche God hath moued me vnto by his gracious inſpiracion. Thou haſt no taſt nor fauour how delicious God is vnto a pure conſcience, in godlye exerſyce of good workes. But all that thou regardeſt and feleſt, is voluptuous pleaſure in worldly vanities. And therfore thou doeſt not perceaue, how that they, which be indued with a ſpeciall grace of God, maye fynde more pleaſure and paſtyme in godly gouernaunce, to keepe togyther, and ſaue ſymple men, then in haukyng and huntynge, to chafe and kyll wylde beaftes. Yea, a godly kyng fhall fynde more pleafure in cafting lottes for Ionas, to try out offenders, whiche trouble the fhip of this commune wealthe, then in caftyng dice at hafarde, to alow and maintayne by his example, fuch thynges as fhulde not be fuffered in a commune wealth. Yea furely, a good Kynge fhall take farre more delyte in edifiyng with conforte and deckyng with good order the Congregacion of his people, the Churche and Houfe of God, the heauenly Citie of Ierufalem, then in buildyng fuche houfes as feeme gaye and gorgeous, and be in deede but vile earthe, ftones, tymber and claye. Suche lyke anfwere ought your Mageftye, and all noble men to make, if ye fynde anye of youre Counfellers more carnall than fpiritual, more worldlye then godly. Orels turne awai your eares from fuche Philippians, and heare other, as Chrift dyd.

Then fayde vnto hym one of his Difciples, Andrew, Symon Peters brother, There is a boy here that hath fiue barley loaues and two fyfhes, but what auayle thofe among fo manye?

Note here that this boye was the Apoftles page, and thefe loaues and fyfhes were their vittayles. For as appeareth in Marke, when he had made fearche how many loaues they them felues had, this anfwer was made, that thei had. v loues and. ii. fifhes : but what be thei amongeft fo many? As who fhulde fay : although thefe be al that euer we haue, and feeme more meete to be kepte amongeft a fewe, then to be gyuen vnto many : yet forbicaufe thei [that] be cum [come], [whiche beyng] many haue more nede then we : yet [therefore] ar we willyng to giue them to be difpofed, and wyffhe that they were of more value to dooe more good amongeft the people.

Thefe men cared more for the Commune people then they dyd for them felues, and therfore were very meete to be Counfellers, and neare about a great Kyng. [And furely none can continue neare, and deare vnto our

kyng Chrift but fuche, for others that euer prolle for priuate profite, bee hypocrites and flatterers as was Iudas.
And] Here wee perceyue what fymple Philip, and good Andrewe thynke, but here is nothing declared of couetous Iudas counfell. No, for Chrift beyng fully purpofed to doo a good deede, dothe neither afke, nor heare any counfell of couetous Iudas: teaching all them which intende any goodnes, neuer to afke nor admit anye counfell of thofe whom thei know to be couetous. For trulye the couetous mans counfell, although it feeme neuer fo good and honeft, yet is it in deede nought and deuelifh. For what could feeme better counfell, then yat a litle ointment, the fwete fmell of the whiche continued but a whyle among a few, fhuld haue ben foulde for. iii. hundreth pence, the great price of the whiche, beftowed amongeft manye poore, fhulde haue done them good for a great ceafon [feafon]?

The Euangelift dothe fhewe howe that Iudas dyd gyue thys counfell, not for that he had anye care of the poore, but becaufe he was a theefe, and baire the bagges.

Iudas pretence was wonders goodly, to fell the oyntment for a great fumme of money, to relieue the poore with: but his purpofe was deuelyfh, to get the money in his bagges, and keepe it to him felfe. And thofe in Englande, which dyd pretende, that befydes the abolyfhynge of fuperfticion, with the landes of Abbeyes, Coliges [Colledges], and Chauntryes, the Kyng fhuld be enriched, learnyng mainteyned, pouertye relieued, and the commune wealth eafed, and by this pretence, purpofely haue enriched theim felues, fettyng abrode incloyftred papiftes, to get their liuyngs by giuyng them penfions, yea, and thruftyng them into benefices to poyfon the whole commune welth for the refignacion of thofe pencions, and fo craftly conueying much from the King, from lernyng, from pouertie, and from all the commune welth, vnto their owne priuate vauntage. Thefe mennes counfell femed better then Iudas counfell was: and their couetoufnes, by their owne deedes appeareth no leffe then Iudas couetoufneffe dyd. Well, beware, for if ye play Iudas part on ftyll, and make no reftitucion, vntil ye go to hangyng, ye ar lyke to fynde defperacion at th[e]ende of your life, bicaufe ye wold not by reftitucion amende your life. Ye noble men, and efpecialli you of the kings counfel, for the reuerence of God, pitie of the commen welth, and fafegarde of your felfes, awaye with thefe Iudaffes, let them go hang them felfes: excepte peraduenture ye thynke yt fytte and neceffary, that you fyrft hang them afore they betray you. For vndoubtedly, he that hath the couetoufnes of Iudas in his hert, he wyll playe all the other partes of Iudas, if he euer haue fuche oportunitie as Iudas had.

Away with Iudas, and learne at Andrew, to faye vnto this kynge and his counfell intendyng to relieue the multitude of his people here in Englande, learne ye noble men to faye: Here is a boye: Here be feruauntes and retainers of ours, which haue fyne loaues and two fyfhes, many benefyces, fome prebendes, with dyuers offices: yea, and fome of vs our felues haue mo offyces then we can difcharge. Pleafeth it your maieftie to take thefe into your handes, which haue ben kepte for vs, that they nowe in this greate nede, may be better difpofed amongeft your people. *Quid hoc inter tantos?*[1] Thefe be verye fmall thynges towardes the amendment of fo many lackes, in fo great a multitude. How be it thefe wyll ferue, fo that there may be mo good Perfons, good Preachers, and good officers placed abrode in euery countrey, whiche in doing their offices, keping of houfes, and preachyng of gods word, may teache the ignoraunt, relieue the poore, punyfh the fau[l]tye, and cheryfh the honeft, and fo repayre the pale of good ordre about this commen welth. For the loue of god gyue your feruauntes wages, and caufe them to reftore thefe liuings, which comyng of the fweate of the labourer, be in dede the reliefe of the poore, ye maintenaunce of honefty, and the reward of vertue, yea, the very pale,

---

[1] John *vi.* 9.

wall, and bulwarkes of the commen wealth. The Apoſtles gaue al that thei had of their own, frely vnto other: ſtycke not you to reſtore yat now which ye haue of long time vncharitably kept from other.

Heare what foloweth: whan theſe fiſhes and loaues were brought vnto Ieſus, make (ſayth he) the people to ſyt doune. God alwaies beſtoweth his benefites vpon them that ſyt doune in quietnes, and powreth furth his vengeaunce vpon thoſe that be vnpacient, vnquiet, and full of buſyneſſe. For as appeareth in Geneſis: The people gathered togither in the plain of Sannaer [Sanner], and made a great vprore, buyldyng a towre lyke rebels againſt god, to get them a name. Howbeit god deſtroyed their handywork, confounded their langage, and ſcatred them abrode.

The Scribes and the Phariſeys came vnquietly, tempting Chriſt, and requyred a ſygne from heauen. Chriſt rebuked them ſharply, and ſhewed them no ſygne, but called them a frowarde and aduoutrous generacion. So the people in Englande gathered togyther, thei woulde make maiſteryes, and bee notable felowes, yea, the towre of their preſumpcion ſhuld be buylt vp vnto heauen, in diſpite of gentyl men and nobilitie: they haue partlye felte, and we haue ryghte pitifully ſeene how ſore God was therwith offended. Now I heare ſaye there is as yet remainyng in England ſum ſtiffe necked Iewes, which come preſumptuouſly tem[p]tyng God, and ſay: if theſe our rulers be ſent of God to take better order then other haue done, well then let theym begynne betyme to gyue vs a notable ſygne and token, for els we wyll not bileeue, truſt, nor obey them.

Well, I wyl tell you that thus whyſper: Euen as Chriſte was *Poſitus in reſurrectionem et ruinam multorum in Iſraell*:[1] Set to reſtore and dekay manye in Iſraell: So be Chriſten rulers in euerye commune wealth, ſet and ordeyned of God, to beate doune and kepe vnder theſe ſturdye rebels, whiche be ſo euyll

---

[1] Luke *ii.* 34.

themfelues, that thei can not thynke that any man doth intende to doo them good, and to reife vp, conforte and cherifh the fimple pacient people, which be of a good truft towards their rulers, knowynge that they themfelfes haue deferued no euil: orels if they haue done euyll, yet by repentaunce and amendment, do not doute to obteyne mercye at their rulers handes. So God hath ordeyned rulers to cheryfhe the[e], if thou be made quiet and pacient, orels to punifh the if you [thou] be vnquiet, bufy, and ftoborne. Learne at [S.] Paul. Ro. xiii. If you do wel, to truft wel of thy rulers, and if thou do euil, not to be without fere of their powers: for he beareth not ye fword without a caufe. Take hede therfore ye rulers, for gods fake, and pitie of the people, feyng yat god hath geuen you a fword, to cut of rotten cankred membres, for ye fafegard of ye hole body, knowing no canker to be fo dangerus as is rebellion in a comen welth: If ye finde one perfon infected with that canker, away with him, for ye fafegard of ye body of yat houfe. If one houfe be infected, away with it, for the fafegard of yat toune. If ye toune be infected, awai with it, for ye fafegard of the contrey. Yea, if a fhyre or contrey be al poyfoned, away with it, for the pitie and fafegarde of the hole body of the comen welth. So ye fe that the fharper yat your fword is, and ye foner that ye ftrike rebellion, ye more pitie ye fhew [fheweye] in cutting awai the leffe, and fauing ye more part and porcion of the people, being al of one body, of one realme and comen welth. Confider that Chrift went from Ierufalem vnto wildernes, to draw ye gentle people from among ye ftoborn fcribes: and fo chriften rulers muft now nedes defer ye time to draw ye people yat be good and truft well, from among this froward generacion, whiche of prefumcion loke to haue ordre taken as they require and appoint ye time, ye place, and ye thing. Wherfore ye yat be good quiet people beware of thefe bufi felowes, and as this multitude which ought to be your example, folowed chrift into wildernes, fo folow you chriſten rulers, gods officers, your chefe gouerners in england. And as thei dyd not murmour, faiing: why ſhal we fyt doune here in wildernes, being an infinit number wher no meat is, feing that in the cities where was more meate, and leſſe gatherynge of the people, we had neuer feaſt gyuen ot hym by his Apoſtles?

So I fay, do not you grudge and faye: why ſhall we quiet our felues nowe, truſtynge to releefe, where wee fee nothyng, and were nothyng at all releeued when there was great plentye of landes, and goodes of Abbeyes, Cole[d]gies, and Chauntries? Do not murmour fo vngodly, but fee that there bee no faulte in you, and ye ſhal fynde no lacke in God. Surely, excepte ye do fytte doune quietly, ye ſhall fooner prouoke Gods vengeaunce to your damnacion, then deferue any releefe of Gods offycers, to your confort. Syt doune and be quiet, for the fame rulers and miniſters are ordeyned of God, to feede you with plentye: whiche be commaunded of God to make you fyrſt to fytte doune in ordre and quietnes. Yea, and herke all ye that be godlye Rulers: there was much graſſe in the place. God had prouided much graſſe for theym that loked for no carpets: geuing all godly gouernours example to prouyde thynges neceſſarye for thofe people that loketh for no fuperfluities. But alas, here in England, fuperfluous gorgeous building is fo much prouided for ryche mens pleafures, that honeſt houfes do decay, where as labouryng men ought to haue neceſſary lodgyng. It is a commen cuſtome with couetous landlordes, to lette their houfynge fo decaye, that the fermer ſhalbe fayne for a fmall rewarde or none at all, to gyue vp his leaſſe, that they takynge the groundes into their owne handes, may turne all to paſture: fo now Olde Fathers, poore Wydowes, and yong Chyldren lye beggyng in the myrie ſtretes.

O mercyfull Lorde, what a numbre of Poore, Feble, Haulte, Blynde, Lame, fycklye, yea, with idle vacaboundes, and diſſemblyng kaityſſes mixt among them, lye and creepe, beggyng in the myrie ſtreates of London and Weſtminſter?

Nowe ſpeakyng in the behalfe of theſe vile beggers, foraſmuche as I know that ye vileſt perſon vpon erth, is the liuely image of almightye God, I wyl tell the[e] that art a noble man, a worſhipful man, an honeſt welthye man, eſpecially if thou be Maire, Shirif, Alderman, baily, conſtable or any ſuch officer, it is to thy great ſhame afore the worlde, and to thy vtter damnacion afore god, to ſe theſe begging as thei vſe to do in the ſtreates. For there is neuer a one of theſe, but he lacketh eyther thy charitable almes [almoſe] to relieue his neede, orels thy due correction to punyſh his faute. A great ſyn and no leſſe ſhame is it for him that ſaith he is a chriſten man, to ſee chriſt lacke things neceſſary, and to beſtow vpon the deuyl ſuperfluoſly. It is Chriſt Ieſu[s] himſelf that in the nedi doth ſuffer hunger, thriſt and colde. It is the deuil him ſelfe, that in the wealthye fareth dientily, goeth gorgiouſly, and vſeth ſuperfluitye. Looke Matthewe the. xxv. and there ſhall ye ſee playnlye that it is Chriſt which lacketh ſufficient in the neadye: and therfore the deuyll beyng contrary to Chriſt, contrariwiſe hath to much in the wealthye.

You alſo that do prouide that your cattell dooe not longe tarye pynned in a folde where there is no graſſe, whye dooe you ſuffer youre owne brethren in Chriſt, withoute prouiſion to lye in the ſtreates, where is muche myer? Theſe ſely fols [ſeelie ſoules] haue ben neglected throghout al England and eſpecially in London and Weſtminſter: But now I truſt that a good ouerſeer, a godly Byſhop I meane, wyl ſee that they in theſe two cyties, ſhall haue their neede releeued, and their faultes corrected, to the good enſample of al other tounes and cities.

Take heede that there be much graſſe to fytte vpon, there as ye commaund the people to ſyt doune, that there be ſufficient houſyng, and other prouiſion for the people there as ye commaunde them to be quiet. The men ſatte doune about fyue thouſandes in number.

If they had not ben obedient to fyt doune, Chriſt wolde not haue ben liberal to haue gyuen theym meate.

Meate was prouided for the Commens of Englande, and ready to haue ben deliuered: But when they were bydden to fyt doune in quietnes, they roſe vp by rebellion, and haue loſt all the chere of that feaſt. Yet that notwithſtandyng, I truſt that thoſe whiche ſat quietly in dede, ſhall ſoone be fedde with plentye, if they fytte ſtyll, vntyll it may conueniently be diſpoſed. I pray God they may, I truſt thei ſhall. The Euangeliſt ſayth that the men ſatte, namyng neither women nor chyldren: how be it there was bothe women and chyldren, as appeareth in the other Euangeliſtes. And men be here named only, bicauſe all women and chyldren dyd folowe the example, and obey the commaundement of men, chyldren of their[the] fathers, and women of their huſbands.

Let not therfore your wyues and chyldren, when they come abrode, be ſo bolde openly, as to ſay or do any thynges of them ſelfes, but as they haue example and commaundement of you. Nowe the multitude placed in quietnes:

Ieſus toke the loaues, and when he had gyuen thankes, he diuided them vnto his Diſciples, and the Diſciples vnto them that were ſet doune: and likewyſe of the fyſhes, ſo muche as they wolde.

Here learne fyrſt of Chriſt, to take nothyng, be it neuer ſo lytell, but with thankes rendered therfore vnto God: For of God ſurely thou haſt receaued it, by what meſſenger or meane ſo euer thou came vnto it. Then ſecondarily, learne at the Apoſtles to giue vnto other, that which the Lord hath gyuen vnto the, that thou mayſt truly ſay with the Apoſtle Paul: *Quod accepi a domino, hoc tradidi vobis*:[1] That whiche I receaued of the Lorde, haue I geuen vnto you. Beware that thou playe not the wycked feruaunt, which kepte his talent hyd, and not deliuered vnto any vſe,

---

[1] 1 Cor. xi. 23.

for then it shall be taken from the, and thou shalte be caste into vtter derkenesse.

Now, to applye this miracle vnto this present time, time, the Kyngs Magestye may learne at Christe, to take of his seruantes, Prebendes, Benefices, Improperacions, and all maner of Offyces, that be not presently occupyed and executed of a faythfull diligent offycer: and after thankes geuen vnto God therfore, to delyuer them vnto his Counsell and Nobilitie, to be disposed amongest the people of his Realme, which be in such hungre and lacke of faythfull offycers, and housekepers, and godly preachers, that thei must needes faint, excepte they be sone prouided for.

And in this distribucion of offyces and benefyces, your Magestye with your Counsell had nede to stande and beholde the dealyng of your nobles, as Christ dyd of his Apostles. For it is not vnlike but as there was amongest Christes Apostles, so wyll there be amongest euerye Christen Kynges Councellers and Nobles, some Iudas, whiche is to be trusted no further than he can be seene. For in syght Iudas dothe as other of his felowes do: but beyng out of syght, he solde his Maister. And so the moste couetous of them all, wyll be a frayde to do any thynge amysse, if you loke vpon: but if your backes be turned, then wyll couetous Iudas sell dearely that which his liberall maister gyueth freely. As for example of late dayes, the Kynges Magesty that dead is. dyd gyue a Benefyce to be appropriate vnto the Vniuersitie of Cambridge, *In liberam et puram elie-mosynam*: As free and pure almes. How be it, his handes were so vnpure, which shuld haue deliuered it, that he receaued. vi. hundred poundes of the Vniuersitye for it. Whether that this. vi.C. pounds were conueied to the kings behoofe priuely for that Almes, which by playne writyng was giuen freely, orels put into some Iudas pouch, I wold it wer knowen. For nowe, by suche charitable Almes, the kyng is slaundered, the parysh vndone, and the Vniuersitye in worse case then it was afore.

Pleaseth it your Mageftye, with your honorable Counsell, for the reuerence of God, the pitie of the poore, and the godlye zele that ye haue to good lernyng, heare what hath ben done in your tyme.

Your Mageftie hath had gyuen, and receaued by Act of Parliament, Coilegies, Chauntries, and guyldes for many good confideracions, and efpecially as appeareth in ye fame Act, for erecting of Grammer fcoles, to the educacion of youthe in vertue and godlynes, to the further augmentyng of the vniuerfyties, and better prouifion for the poore and needye. But nowe, many Grammer fcholes, and much charitable prouifion for the poore, be taken, folde, and made awaye, to the great flaunder of you and your lawes, to the vtter difconforte of the poore, to the greuous offence of the people, to the moft miferable drounynge of youthe in ignoraunce, and fore decaye of the Vniuerfities.

There was in the North countrey, amongeft the rude people in knowledge (which be moft readye to fpende their lyues and goodes, in feruyng the Kyng at the burnyng of a Beacon) there was a Grammer fchole founded, hauyng in the Vniuerfitie of Cambridge, of the fame foundacion, viii. fcholerfhips, euer replenyfhed with the fcholers of that fchole, which fcole is now folde, decayed, and lofte. Mo there be of lyke forte handled: But I recyte thys only, bicaufe I knowe that the fale of it was once ftayed of charitie, and yet afterwards broughte to paffe by bribrye, as I hearde fay, and beleue it, bicaufe that it is only bribrye, that cuftomablye ouercometh charitie.

For Gods fake, you that be in aucthoritie, loke vpon it.

For if ye winke at fuche matters, God wyl fcoule [that is to faie, looke with anger vppon you] vpon you. Thinke not that I do burden you with more than that, which God by his ordynance, not without your willes and confentes, hath charged you withall. For by whofe fau[l]t[e] or negligence fo euer it was, that things afore tyme haue ben vncharitablye abufed, furelye it is youre charge, whiche be now in

F

aucthoritie, to fe at this tyme all fuche thynges as yet remain out of ordre, rightoufly, fpedely, and charitably redreffed. And as I do perceiue, that the abufe of thefe thynges afore tyme, hath offended God, troubled the commen wealthe, and brought fome men towardes fhame and confufion : So do I wyfh, pray, and trufte, that now the redreffe of the fame, may be to Gods pleafure, the peoples confort, and to the honor and eftablyfhment of theym that be in moft hygh aucthoritie.

Heare therfore, and I wyll tell you more: There were in fome townes. vi. fome. viii. and fome a dozen kyne, gyuen vnto a flocke, for the reliefe of the poore, and vfed in fuch wyfe, that the poore cotingers, which coulde make any prouifion for fodder, had ye mylke for a very fmall hyre: and then the number of the flocke referued, all maner of vailes befydes, bothe the hyre of the mylke, and the pryces of the yonge veales, and olde fat wares, was difpofed to the reliefe of the poore, thefe be alfo folde, taken, and made away. The Kyng beareth the flaunder, the poore feeleth the lacke, but who hath the profit of fuche thynges, I can not tell: but well I wot, and all the worlde fayth, that the Act of Parliament made by the Kynges Mageftye, and his Lords and Commens of the Parliament, for the mayntenaunce of learnyng, and reliefe of the poore, hath ferued fome, as a moft fyt inftrument to robbe learnyng, and to fpoyle the poore. If you that be now in aucthoritie do not loke vpon fuch thynges to redreffe them, God wyl loke vpon you, to reuenge theim. Here haue I reherfed them, that the Kynges Mageftye, with you of his counfell maye learne, not onlye by the doctrine and examples of fcripture, but alfo by experience in his owne lande, to fee and confyder howe his benefytes, put into the handes of his nobles and officers, be difpofed and vfed amongeft his inferioure people.

For if landed men and officers, by keping of houfes, and doing of their dutyes in their countryes, do beftowe amongeft [emong] the people, all that they haue receaued of God, by the kynges gyft, their fathers inheritaunce, or other wayes: then shall God giue such increase, that euery man shall haue inough.

As Salomon, the. xi. of the Prouerbes testifieth: *Alii diuidunt propria, et ditiores fiunt: alii rapiunt non sua, et semper in egestate sunt*:[1] Some dispose and gyue their owne, and become rycher and rycher: some doo raueyn and spoyle that which is not their owne, and be euer in lacke and neede. As ye see in dailye experience, those that do their owne dutyes in executynge their offyces, and bestowe theire owne goodes in keepyng good houses, haue euer suche plentye, that all other men meruayle from whence God sendeth it. And those that dooe no duties, nor keepe no houses, but brybe in their offyces, and polle their tenauntes, take so much, and haue so lytell, that all men wunder how the deuyl thei wast it.

Nothyng is more true than the gospel: *Date, et dabitur vobis*:[2] Gyue and it shall be gyuen vnto you. Giue plentifully vnto other, and God wyl gyue more plentye vnto you. For God wyll alwayes be afore hande, in giuynge good gyftes. For as appeareth in this gospell, when the Apostles had giuen vnto the people so much good meate as they desyred, then sayeth the Euangelist:

When thei were filled, Iesus fayeth to his disciples: Gather vp the broken meates that remayn, so that nothynge be lost. They therfore gathered, and fylled .xii. baskets ful with the broken meates remaining of that which they had eaten.

Here they gaue but. v. loaues and .ii. fyshes, and there was gyuen vnto them. xii. baskets ful of meats.

The Wydowe of Sareptha, gaue but one handfull of flowre, and a lytle oyle vnto Elias, and had gyuen vnto her agayne so muche as serued her and her sonne, al the tyme of the greate droughte .iii. Re[gu]. xvii. Learne therfore that couetous bribry and extorcion hath neuer ynough: and charitable liberalitie, euer hathe plentye. Here also maye ryche men learne, when and howe to

---

[1] Prov. *xi.* 24.   [2] Luke *vi.* 38.

fyll their ſtore houſes. Surelye, euen as the Apoſtles dyd fyll their baſkettes, when the people haue [had] ynoughe, then by gatheryng vp that which els ſhoulde be loſt. So dyd Ioſephe in Egipt, ſuffre no corne to be loſt in the yeares of plenty, but ſtored it vp in barnes, to relieue the people with, in ye tyme of darth: Not as couitous carles do here in Englande forſtall the markettes, and b[u]ye corne at all tymes, to begynne and encreaſe a dearth. Bleſſed be they that ſell, to make good cheape, and curſed be they that b[u]ye, to make it deare. For Salomon ſayeth, Prouerb. xi. *Qui abſcondit frumenta, maledicetur in populis : benedictio autem ſuper caput vendencium :*[1] He that hydeth vp corne, ſhall be curſed amongeſt the people: But bleſſyng be vpon their heades, that ſell.

Nowe, to teache Chriſten rulers their dutyes, in the example of Chriſtes Apoſtles: marke how the Apoſtles dyd fyrſt miniſter vnto the people, and than gathered vp for them ſelfes: teachyng therby all Chriſten miniſters, landelordes, offycers, and rulers, fyrſte to miniſter vnto the people, euery one the dutye of his owne vocacion, afore they gather of the people, rentes, tythes, or fees, by the name and aucthoritie of that vocacion. *Qui non laborat,* ſayth [S] Paul, *non manducet :*[2] He that doth not labour, ſhuld not eate. He that doth no worke, ſhulde take no wages: he that dothe no dutyes, ſhoulde take no fees. Alas, this is Gods woorde, written in his wylle and Teſtament, ſealed with Chriſtes bloude, and yet the cuſtomes and lawes of Englande be cleane contrarye. For it hath ben cuſtomeably vſed, yea, and by lawes commaunded, to paye wages, tythes, and fees, although no labour, no offyce, no dutye be done. Yea, although he be not a labourer, a paſtor, or an offycer in dede, but only by a pretenſed name, vnto whom theſe for the moſt parte be payed.

For he that hath the properties, and vſeth the trades of a falſe theſe, and a cruell murtherer, can neuer be a faythful offycer in dede, altho[u]gh he be ſo named by

---

[1] Prov. *xi*. 28.   [2] 2 Theſs. *iii*. 10

his owne flatery, in the Patrons prefentacion, in the Byfhoppes induction, yea, and in the Kynges Patent, fealed with the brode Seale. I had nede to take heede howe that I fpeake openly agaynft any thyng in any mans Patent, fealed with the kings greate Seale: Muche more nede had you to take heede, how that ye do any thyng expreffedly agaynft Gods wyll and Teftament, fealed with Chriftes precious bloude. It is expreffedly agaynfte Gods Teftament, to clothe a Wolfe in a Lambes fkynne: to call a thefe, an officer: and a cruel murtherer, a charitable paftor: to call euyll, by the name of good: and good, by the name of euyll. Efaye. v. *Væ qui dicitis malum bonum*:[1] Wo be to you that cal euyl good. To you I fay, which not only by fayings, but alfo in writynges, do name and cal thieues, murtherers, and wolfes that be euyll, by the names of officers, paftors, and lambes, which be good. I dooe not only meane, Perfones, Prebendaries, and other benefifed men, but alfo all maner of* officers, which haue wages, fees, or lyuynges, bicaufe you gyue them fuche names, and not for that thei do fuche dutyes.

Thefe be al Wolfes, and the names and tytles that you gyue them, be nothyng els but fheepe fkynnes. Some faye, they wyll take better heede here after, but that which is now paft, can not nowe be called backe, and amended. Yea, and it were great pitie, feeyng that they haue payed the fyrft fruites vnto the Kynges Mageftie, and no fmall reward vnto other men, perchaunce bought their offices dearely, now to put them out of thofe liuyngs, with the loffe of all thofe charges, whiche they haue beftowed in rewardes, as otherwayes, to gette fuche liuynges.

Wo, wo, wo vnto you hipocrites that ftumble at a ftrawe, and leape ouer a blocke, that ftrayne out a gnat, and fwalowe vp a camell, that pitye more the loffe of mens bribrye, which was geuen to corrupt fome men, than the treding vnder fote of Chriftes blood, which was fhead, to faue all men, that dooe imagen it pitie to driue the theues, murtherers and

---

[1] Isa. v. 20.

wolfes from amongeſt the lambes of God, redemed with Chriſtes precious blood, and committed vnto your gouernaunce and kepynge.

As God ſhal help me, I ſpeake with feare, pitie, and reuerence: if you do not rather pulle the ſhepes ſkines ouer the wolfes eares, and hange their carkaſes vpon the pales, than ſuffer theim to contynewe ſtyll, God wyll plucke you doune with ſome ſodeyn miſchief, rather than mainteyn or ſuffer you in ſo hygh aucthoritie, to vſe ſuch vncharitable, vngodly, and cruel pitie. You knowe that ſome of them haue bought their benefices, haue bought theire offyces, than muſt ye nedes knowe, that eyther Chriſt is a lyer, orels that they be entered in as theeues, to ſpoyle, murther, and to deſtroye.

If you ſuffre theeues, murtherers, and wolfes, to take their pleſures amongeſt Gods lambes, I tell you playn, God wyll not long ſuffer you to be ye hedſhepherds, and gouernors and feders of his lambes.

And take hede you people, that on the other ſyde ye runne not into an vntollerable ſtobornes, deniing your rents, your tithes or other duties: for ye ſcriptur forbiddeth you vtterly, to deny or withdraw any thing from them: thou art commaunded if he contend to take thi cloke, to giue him alſo thy cote. What ſo euer is aſked, rather gyue more, than by denying of that, not to ſhewe thy ſelfe to be an innocent ſheepe that gyueth his fleeſe, but a noyſome Goat, that ſtryketh with the horne. You are alwayes bounden to gyue the fleeſe. It is magiſtrates dutyes, to confyder and note, whether they be theeues, or ſhepheardes, dogges. or wolfes that taketh the fleeſe. Medle not with other mens dutyes, for if ye do, ſurely ye ſhal fynd no remedy, but prouoke vncolourable [vntollerable] vengeaunce.

Now to retourne [turne] to our particular purpoſe, let all theym that do receaue offices, landes, power, or aucthoritie from God, by the kyngs gyfte, or by other meanes: Fyrſt beſtow and diſpoſe the dutyes of thoſe thyngs faythfully amongeſt the people, afore they gather vp to them felues the reuenues amd commodities of the fame from the people. And then, when as no man can come to meat, but by doing of labour, nor none to receauynge of fees, but by doing of duties, furely euery man fhal haue as much as he deferueth, and no man fhall lacke that which he needeth.

For he, that by doyng of great duties deferueth the mofte, by atteinynge the fees and rewardes due for the fame dutyes, fhall haue the beft. And he that is in nede, hauing no truft to get any thyng by idleneffe, craft, or flattery, fhalbe compelled to vfe that labour and honeft exercife, whiche fhall relieue his nede fufficiently. Yea, by this mean no man fhall fpende his tyme in idleneffe, nor vfe no [any] labour or diligence, without due recompence. For nede fhall driue all men from flouthfull idleneffe, vnto labour and diligence: and where as no labour nor diligence lacketh his iuft rewarde, there euery labouryng and diligent man, fhal haue fufficient plenty. So ye fee how this doth confequently enfue, that euery man fhall haue fufficient inough and plentie, where as men do firft difpofe and minifter, and giue according to their duties, and afterwards receiue, kepe and faue that which God doth fende as a rewarde, encreafed and augmented, for doyng of their dutyes.

So dyd the Apoftles, after the faythful diligent difpofyng of the. v. loaues and. ii. fyfhes, receyue and keepe their rewarde wonderfullye augmented, to replenifh and fyl. xii. bafkets. So God graunt, that all officers in Englande, may with fuch faithful diligence do their duties. yat it may pleafe God to giue to all the people fufficient enough, and vnto euery minifter, the bafket of his honeft defire, heped vp by ye brym.

The men therefore feyng what a fygne Iefus had done, fayd that this is ye Prophet, whiche cometh vnto [into] the world. This is euen he whom Moifes, the

law, and the prophetes do teache, to be the fullye and
only fufficient fauiour of ye world. Moifes faiing, in
ye. xviii. of Deut. A Prophet of thy nacion and of thy
brethren, lyke vnto me, fhall the Lorde thy God rayfe
vp vnto the, him fhalt thou heare. The lawe, as a
tutour, leadeth and bryngeth al men to this fauyour,
to receaue of him that perfection, which the law it
felfe lacketh. The Prophetes dyd tel long afore of
this fauiour, which is now comen in our tyme, after
their dayes. This was the peoples confeffion of
Chrift, after that they were by fo great a miracle, fo
plentifully fed. Chrift, ofte afore had wrought wonderfull miracles, difputed learnedly, and preached
plainly: but by all thofe meanes dyd he not fo muche
perfwade the people, and wynne their heartes, as by
this one miracle, in feedyng and cherifhing the people.
Yea, and whofoeuer lifteth to mark thorow out all
England, he fhall fee that a meane learned perfon,
keping an houfe in his paryfh, and kepynge of godly
conuerfacion, fhall perfwade and teach mo of his
parifhioners with communicacion at one meale, than
the beft lerned doctor of diuinitie kepyng no houfe,
can perfwade or teache in his parifh by preaching a
dofen folemne fermons.

Lykewyfe the gentle man that kepeth a good houfe
in his countrey, fhall be in better credit with the
people for his liberalitie, than the beft oratour or
lawyer in England, for all his eloquence. I do not
prayfe thofe men which brybe and polle all the yeare
to kepe riot in their houfes for a fortnyght, a moneth,
or a quarter of a yeare: But thofe I fe be loued,
trufted, and obeyed, that accordynge to their habilitie,
keepe good houfes continually.

And the chiefe caufe why the commens doo not
loue, truft, nor obey the gentle men and officers, is,
bicaufe the gentle men and officers buyld many fayre
houfes, and kepe few good houfes, haue plentye of
eloquence to tell fayre tales, but vfe lytell faythfull

diligence in doyng of their duties. Wherfore, fende forth, and place in euery countrey godly preachers, wel difpofed perfons [Parfones], and faithfull diligent officers, of all fortes. Yea, but where fhuld we now fynd liuyngs for al thofe.

For foth I do tell you: Out and away with the wily foxes, the falfe flatteryng theeues, and the rauening wolfes, and than fee how many loaues, how many offyces, prebends, and benefices ye finde voyde, how many you haue amongeft your felues that your boye caryeth, that your chapleyns, your feruauntes, and your houfeholde offycers haue, and let all thefe be brought forth: and althoughe at the fyrft fyght they fhall feeme to lytell, and few to ferue fo great a Realme with fo manye fhyres, beyng all runne nowe out of ciuil ordre into rude wildernes. Yet, after equal diuidyng and faithfull diligent miniftrynge of thefe [thofe] loaues and fifhes, of thefe prebends, perfonages, and all kynde of offyce[r]s amongeft the people, God of his goodneffe fhall giue fuch encreafe vnto the people, hauynge therby fufficient plenty of Chriftes holy word, of good ciuil ordre, and of charitable relief, than there fhalbe remainyng fo much tythes, offryng, rentes, fees, and rewards, as wyl fyl the xii. bafkets of the Apoftles, I meane the barnes, the houfes, and purfes of all faythfull diligente minifters and officers. Then fhal this one acte perfwade and allure the herts of all Englifh men more then all that euer was done afore: For when they fhall fee, that by this Kyng and this Counfell, the wilye foxe of fuperfticion is vtterly banyfhed, the falfe theefe of flattery apprehended and taken, and the cruell wolfe of couetoufneffe flayne, and hanged vp by the heeles, fo that the preachers, the perfons, the officers, and all maner of paftors reftored to their places, doo feede, cherifh, and kepe their flockes, which were afore pilled, fpoiled and deuoured: then fhall they of herty courage, with one mynde, and one voyce confeffe and acknowledge, that there [this] is a

King ſent from God, indued with the wyſdome of Salomon, and the faythfull diligent ſtoutneſſe of Dauid his
father, now guyded by godly counſell, to bring out of
miſerye, and proſper in welth vs the people
of this his* Realme.
Dixit Dominus.
The Lord hath
ſpoken it.
God graunt you grace to
do it, with thankes and
prayſe to hym
for euer.

¶ Imprinted
at London by Jhon
Daie, dwelling ouer Al=
derſgate, and Wyl=
liam Seres dwel=
ling in Peter
Colledge.
The yere of our Lorde God
M. D. L. the nynth
daye of Apryll.

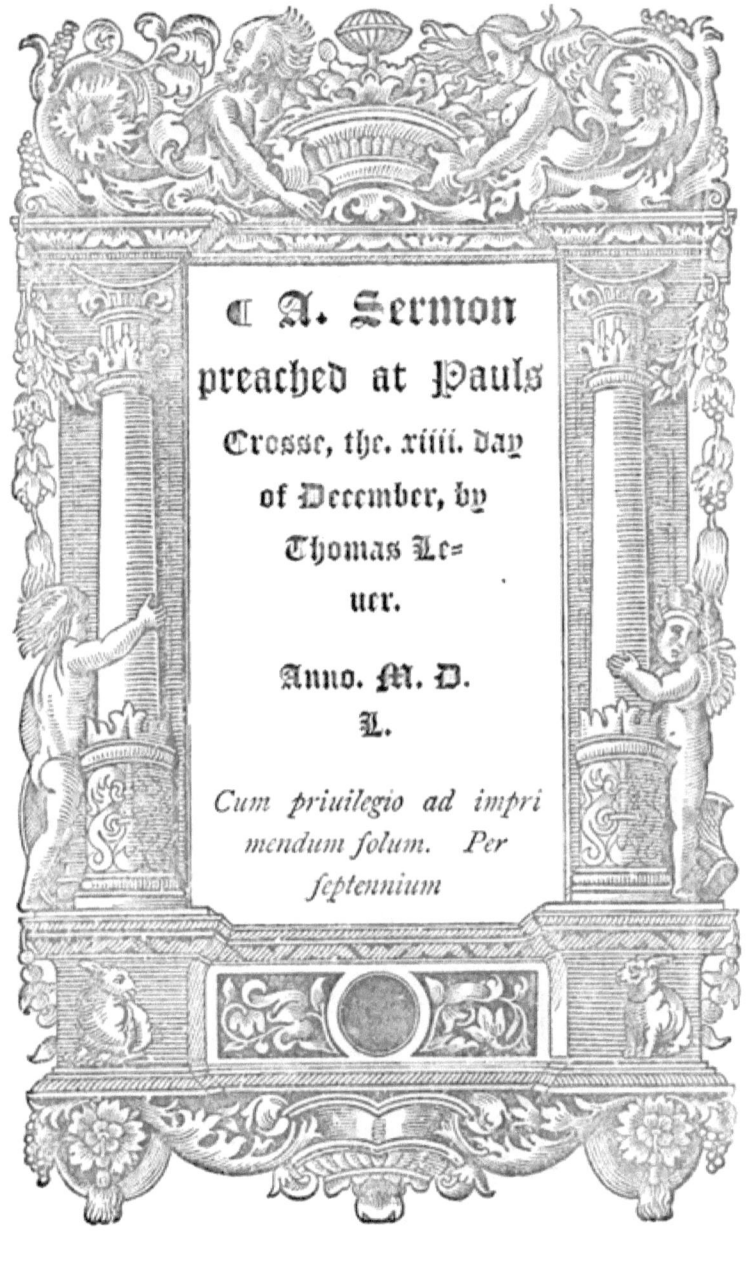

¶ A Sermon preached at Pauls Crosse, the. xiiii. day of December, by Thomas Leuer.

Anno. M. D. L.

Cum priuilegio ad imprimendum solum. Per septennium

¶ Unto the right honor=
rable Lordes, and others of the
Kynges Magestie hys priuye Coun=
sell, Thomas Leauer wysheth in=
crease of Grace and godly
honoure.

Ercy, grace, and peace from God the father almyghty, vnto your honours, wyth my moste humble and reuerente comendacions.

The enemye of God and man alwayes sekyng lyke a rorynge lion whome he may deuoure, is much at al tymes, but then especially to be taken hede vnto, when as he hym self beyng transformed into the aungell of lyght, doth cloke the ministers of hys myschiefe in a pretensed shew of godlines and vertue, so that therby they be suffered of al men, and maynteined of many men, to worcke and brynge vnto passe a deuillishe dysorder, and shamefull dyshonestye in a Christen commen wealth.

Wherefore, seynge that in thys realme preachers, officers, marchauntes, crafts men, labourers, and such lyke, be displaced of their roumes, and dysapoynted of theyr lyuinges by those whych through a pretensed name, and outward apperance, seme to be necessary and profytable ministers in a common wealthe (howbeit in theyr owne doynges may be euidently tryed and knowen for to be spoylers and disturbers of any common welth) suredly you of the kynges most honourable counsell, beyng the chefe maiestrats and rulers in this realme, had nede to be ware, circumspect and diligent, lest that Sathan banyshyng al faithful Christians, whych should and wold prouyde to helpe one an other, do fyl this realme ful of crafty flatterers, whych can and wyll deceyue, begyle, and fpoyle one another.

Truly ther be no men more againft Chrift then thofe which by profeffion of Chriften relygyon, and bearyng of a Chriften name, doo rob Chryft of hys honor, and Chriftes minifters of theyr liuyngs: nor none more parilous ennemies vnto the kings maiefty, and vnto this realme, then thofe whyche haue the names of Englifh-men, and the kyngs fubiects with ye condicions and maners of enemies, and traitors.

Moft gracious good lordes and maifters, for your reuerent loue towardes God, and the kyng, for your charitable pytye of myferable fpoiled people, and for the neceffary regarde of your owne honours, and the ftate of thys realme, fe and confyder how that ambicious couetous men, do bye and fel, take and abufe perfonages, prebendes, offyces, fees, marchaundyfe, fermes, landes, and goodes, fo that prowlyng for them felues, they be neither afrayde, nor afhamed to fpoile thys realme of preachyng of Gods gofpel, of iuftyce and equitie, of cheape and plenty, and of euery thynge that fhould faue, kepe, or profytte a commune wealthe.

Wherfore moft gracious good lordes, and mayfters, for the tender mercies of God in our Sauiour Iefus Chrift, take hede that neyther feruaunte, nor frende, reteyner, nor youre felues do deceyue you wyth flatterye.

For feynge that ambicious couetous men do take, kepe, and enioye the roumes and lyuynges of euerye mannes vocacion, bothe you and we be in farre more daunger, then yf blockehoufes and bulwarkes made and kepte of the kynges faythful fubiectes for the fauegarde of thys realme, were taken and abufed of fuche Scottes or Frenchemen, as makyng fpoyle for theyr owne profit, would not fpare to dyftroye thys realme.

There is very manye rowmes and lyuynges, belongynge both vnto the ecclefiaftical mynifterye, and alfo vnto cyuyll policye, in the whyche be no fayethful fubiectes, godlye diligente minifters and offycers, whiche by doynge of theyr duties, doo faue, kepe and comforte the people: but couetous Idolatours, whych neglectyng theyr dutyes, and takynge commodities, doo dyforder, fpoyle and dyftroye the people.

Suerlye if there be any men that goo aboute to perfwade the Kynges Mageftye, or you of hys honourable Councell, that thinges in thys realme for the moft parte be honourablye, godlye, or charytably reformed, they be but flaterers.

For papiftry is not banyfhed out of Englande by pure religion, but ouerrunne, fuppreffed and kepte vnder within thys realme by couetous ambicion. Papiftrye abufed many thyngs, couetoufnes hath diftroyed more: papiftry is fuperfticion, couetoufnes is Idolatry. Papiftrye afore tyme dyd obfcure the Kinges honour, and abufe the wealth of this realme, couetoufnes at thys tyme doth more abufe and decaye theym bothe, makynge the kynge bare, the people poore, and the realme miferable.

The Kynges procedynges to be red in his lawes, ftatutes, and Iniunccions be good and godly: but to be fene and knowen in the dedes and practifes of his officers, feruauntes, and fubiectes, be vngodly, fhameful, wicked. For in theyr doynges appeareth no retournynge from euil vnto good, by a godly reformacion: but a procedyng from euyl vnto worfe, by an vncharitable fpoyle, and deuyllyfhe deftruccion.

Landes and goodes be fpoyled: prouyfyon made for learning and pouerty, is deftroied. Ye knowe in whofe handes thys ryche fpoyle remaineth, then can ye not be ignoraunt by whofe meanes the wealth of this realme is fpoyled and decayed.

If ye wyll haue a godlye reformacion effectuouflye to procede, trufte not the feruauntes of Mammon, ennemyes vnto God, and traitoures vnto the kynge, and fpoylers of the people, wyth the fettyng forthe of your godlye lawes, ftatutes and ordynaunces, which be moft contrary vnto theyr couetous myndes, and wycked dedes.

Theyr myndes are alwayes euyll, and theyr dedes be well knowen, when as you geue frelye, or fuffer theym by brybery to by vnto theim felues authorytye: for then, being trufted to make better prouifion for the pore, to erect mo Grammer fchooles, to encreafe and augment the vnyuerfities, and to fe the people taught louyngly, to reuerence, ferue, and obey God, the kyng, and you: they take prouifyon frome the poore, they fell awaye Grammer fcoles, they decai the vniuerfities, and they vfe fuche practifes, as maketh God to be vnknowen, the kynge dyfobeyed, and you fufpected, hated, and enuyed of the people.

Take thefe falfe flatterers whyche haue enryched them felues, makynge the kynge bare, and the people poore, reftore theyr landes and goodes vnto the kynge, theyr rowmes and offyces vnto faythfull and true offycers and minifters: and then fhal the kyng be enryched, the realme vnfpoyled, and the people delyuered from myferable captiuitie vnder cruel extorcioners, vnto an honeft lybertye vnder Godlye gouernoures, whyche fhall fo dyfpofe the hartes and myndes of all people, that they wyllynglye fhall be readye, not onlye to ferue the markettes wyth corne, but alfo to ferue God and the kynge with landes and gooddes, bodyes and lyues, when and where fo euer you fhal commaunde it.

Maruel not thoughe a faythful hearte, wyth humble obedyence and reuerente loue towardes the kynges Maieftye, and you of hys honourable Godly counfel, do barft [burfte] and poure [put] foorthe a lamentable complaynte of greuous forrowe conceyued in feeynge the kyng fhamefully begyled, you fore difhonored, and the wealthe of thys realme vtterly fpoyled.

For menne dooe bye offyces vnto them felues, and landes from the kynge: and by the onlye fpoyle that is made in common offyces and vpon the kynges landes, bothe thefe bargens be payed for, and furthermore all fuch bargeyners wonderfullye enryched.

O mercyfull Lorde, what a griefe is it vnto a faythfull harte, hauinge iuft occafyon to fufpecte, that you lacke faythful counfell to aduertyfe you of the gracious workynge of the Lorde beynge God, and of the freyle

fautes of youre felues beynge menne, in all youre
doynges: for Gods grace woorkynge in you, caufeth
you to dooe honourable and Godlye feruyce to god,
the kynge, and the common wealthe, when as ye caufe
an vngodly byfhop to be depofed. And yet fhall God,
the king, and the people be greuoufly offended, and
your honors and fowles fo ar indaungered, yf a bifhops
landes or goodes be deuyded amongft you that be
godlye magyfetrates to punyfh euyl doers, as Chriftes
cote was deuyded amongeft wycked foldyers, which
dyd cruelly torment a righteous perfon.

Alas moft gracious reuerente Lordes and mayfters,
if ye vfe the feruyfe, or hear the aduyfe of falfe crafty
flatterers, ye fhall therewyth be fo blynded that ye can
neyther perceyue by your felues, nor beleue when as ye
be playnely and faythfully tolde, that manye of your owne
doynges, commyng of mans freyltye, do tend muche vnto
the difpleafure of God, dyfhonour of the kynge, and
dyfcredyt of your felues, beyng moft contrarye to that
reuerent zele and faythful loue towards God, the kyng,
and the commen wealth, which zele and loue god of hys
goodnes hath grafted in your hartes, and the deuyll by
mannes freyl dedes couered in fylence or colored with
prayfe of flatterers, laboreth to deface, peruert and
deftroye.

As God whyche fearcheth the fecretes of mans hart,
doth beare me recorde, I do fuppofe, and thynke that
you dooe fo louynglye drede God, reuerence the kyng,
and regarde this realme, and your owne honors, that
beyng charged wyth the ouerfight and prouifion of
caftels, holdes, and fortes, made and kept for the fafegarde of thys realme, ye coulde not wyttyngly be hyred
to fell one of them vnto the kynges ennemyes, for al
the treafures in the world. And yet beyng craftelye
deceyued wyth flattery, ye vfe a daungerous practyfe
in very many of them.

For ther be fome of them fclenderly affauted at
certayne tymes of feble enemyes: and other continuallye befeged eyther wyth open forfe or craftye con-

ueyaunce of fearce, cruel, and perylous enemies. And now crafty flatterers whych haue once ferued for theyr wages in tyme and place of the fclender affalte, doo afterwardes requyre and perfwade you for that feruyfe to geue them the fpoyle of other holdes remayning continuallye in more daunger. Truly Frenchmen and Scottes be but feble ennemyes, and [yet] at certayne tymes do fclenderly affalt caftels, towers, and fuch maner of holdes. The deuyl feking lyke a roryng Lyon, whom he may deuoure, nyghte and day, wynter and fommer, wyth a wonderful forfe of wycked fpirites, doth euer befyege byfhopryckes, fhyres, townes, and parifhes.

Yf thefe places be not wel furnifhed with ftout and true foldiers of bothe the fortes (I meane both officers in ciuyle polycy, and alfo Prelates in Ecclefiafticall miniftery) or if thofe fouldyers be vnprouided of neceffary liuyngs and dewe wages, then muft the people nedes peryfhe and be deftroyed for theyr owne fynnes, and the bloud of theyr bodyes and foules requyred at your handes, whyche be charged and trufted of both God, and the king to prouide fouldiers to thofe places, and alfo wages and liuinges to mayntayne thofe foldyers continually.

How be it now* manye perfonages, benefyces, offyces, and fees be fold vnto couetous brybers for money, whych feke nothyng but the vantage of* extorcion, robbry and fpoyle, and fewe of them be freely giuen vnto faithful minifters and officers for their woorthynes, which could and would by diligent doynge of their dutie, gouerne, inftruct and cheryfhe goddes people, the kynges fubiectes.

And therefore nowe the moft part of men lackyng teachers and rulers, do without griefe of confcience, or feare of punifhment, abufe euery thynge vnto the ruine and deftruccion, whyche God hath ordayned vnto the vpholdyng and increafe of a chriftian commune welth.

As for example, now bying and fellyng is not vfed as a prouifion for good cheape and great plenty, but made the moft occafyon of dearth and fcarfitie.

Wealth and wyt be not ryghtly vfed vnto a common confortable profyt, but fhamefully abufed vnto a wycked priuate gayne. Many offyces with authoritie be not duely difpofed vnto faithful worthy men nor to dooe good vnto other, but vnlawfullye bought and folde amongeft couetous, ambicious men, to get gaynes vnto theim felues. So this realme is fpoyled, the kynge is made bare, and his faithful true fubiectes be many of them very poore: but crafti deceiuers, couetous Extorcioners, brybynge offycers, and fuche falfe flatterers be wonderous rich and welthy.

Thefe Flatterers be wonders perilous felowes, hauynge two faces vnder one hoode. For they beare a face and fhew towardes the people, as though by Commyffion and commaundement from you, there muft bee more required and taken of the people then euer you dyd meane or thynke: And towardes you thei fhewe another face femyng that fo much cannot be founde in anye mennes handes as muft needes bee procured: but that therefore the kynges landes muft nedes be folde, whyche thei are redye to by for their owne auantage, wyth thofe goodes whyche they them felues haue in theyr owne handes, or rather wyth the fpoyle whych they intend to make vpon thofe landes. Thefe fubiects that be not afhamed to procure vnto them felues fuch riches, that they maye be biers, and vnto their liege Lorde and kyng fuche nede, that he mufte be a feller of his landes. Thefe be in deede feruauntes vnto Mammon, enemies vnto god, traitores vnto the king, and difturbers of a common welth turning all your godly, wife and charitable deuyces for neceffary prouyfyon, vnto deuylifh deceytes, for to caufe and maynteyne vncharitable fpoyles. And furedly when as occafions do ferue for any men to practife theyr pleafures, manye men of al fortes, and of the loweft fort, the moft part do fhew them felues the worft infected wyth thys impyety, treafon, and rebellyon, the greuoufnes and daunger of the whyche wyth occafyons and meanes how to auoyd the fame, I preaching at

Paules Croffe the. xiiii. [fowertene] day of December laſt paſt, dyd there openly declare vnto mine audience. And as I did then preach that Sermon as an exhortacion to moue the people, by the acknowledgyng, lamentyng and amendynge theyr owne fautes, to deſerue and receyue the pardon of mercy offered vnto them of both god and the kyng, in thys longe pacient fufferaunce, fo do I nowe here offer vnto your honors, the fame Sermon as an earneſt complaynte, to procure of you that be Gods offycers, fpedyly correccion for them that refuſe to heare, regarde, and obey Gods word.

Be not dyſcouraged in thys matter, wyth your owne freylty beyng greate, or wyth the number of offenders, beyng manye. For it is not your worthynes, but Goddes grace, that hath placed you in hygh authority, and in the fame aucthoritye not your owne powers and polycy, but the myght and wifdome of god, fhal fo ſtrengthen and confyrme you, that yf ye wyll be dyligent, ye fhall be made able to delyuer Gods people, the kynges fubiectes, oute of the handes of fuche as be Gods and the kynges ennemyes.

I befeche the almyghtye God indue you wyth grace, that begynnyng wyth youre felues, ye may fpedely procede vnto the neceffary and godly correccion of other mens fautes, fo that ye maye be eſtablyſhed in youre rowmes, and increafed in honor, to ferue god and the kynge, prouiding for hys realme in holines and righteoufnes al ye daies of your lyues.

By me humbly subiect and faithful obedient vnto your honors, Thomas Leuer.

Iesus Christus.

ℂ The grace of the holy gost, procedyng from God the father, by the intercession and meane of Iesu Christ, so prepare your herts, and open my mouth, that I maye declare, and shewe, and that you maye heare, vnderstand, remember, and practise in your liuyng, his liuely word as may be most to his honour and glori and to your soules health and comfort.

Ou Citizins of London, and all other that be here prefent marke, note, and remember what ye heare of me this day: for yf I shall say or speake any thynge that is euyll, you muste beare recorde against me of that euyl. But if I do preache well and truelye, then you shall vnderstande and knowe your selues to be in great daunger of haynous treason towards god and the kinges maiesty of this realme, which be by you spoyled, and robbed: god of his glory, the kyng of hys honoure, and the realme of hys wealth. Howbeit the mercyfull goodnes of bothe god and the kyng hath sent me hyther thys daye, to proclame a generall pardon, intendynge thereby to try out and saue theim that haue offended by simple ignoraunce, becaufe the force of theyr myghty power is nowe readye and commynge vtterly to destroye all other that continue in wylfull stobernes and rebellyous treason. Wherefore afore the readynge of my commyssion, I wyll declare that piece of scriptur whyche appoynted to be red in the churche as thys daye, wyll certyfye you that God by his scriptures hath shewed the kynge, who be hys fayethfull seruauntes, and who be hys ennemyes. Thys scripture is wrytten

in ye. iiii. Chapter of the firſte epiſtle of. S. Paule vnto
the Corinthians. *Sic nos æſtimet homo ut miniſtros
Chriſti, et diſpenſatores miniſtrorum [myſteriorum] dei. etc.*[1]

Filioli mei quos iterum parturio.[2] Albeit I vſe not
ſcrupuloullye the ſame termes, yet conuenyently folowyng
the maner and phraſe of ſcrypture, I ſay vnto you as
Paule wryteth vnto the Galathyans: My deare chyldren
of whom I trauell in byrthe agayne vntyll Chriſte be
facyoned in you, I would I now beyng wyth you
myght chaunge my voyce, whyche heretofore I haue
vſed: declarynge by the worde of God, that you here
in England whych wyll receyue no mercye, ſhall feele
ſore vengeaunce, which wyll not be ſaued, ſhalbe
deſtroyd. Thys voyce vſed here afore of me, nowe
wold I fayne chaunge. For nowe ἀποροῦμαι ἐν ὑμῖν I
doute I am paſte hope and allmooſte in vtter dyſpayre
of you. Tell me you that throughe couetouſnes deſyre
the ryches and wealthe of thys world. Haue ye not
heard how that he whych wold be a frend vnto the
world is made an enemy vnto God, doethe not Paule
teache that couetouſnes is the roote of all euyl? Is it
not wrytten that couetouſnes is Idolatry? Haue ye
not red in the prophet Ezechiel howe that he whyche
kepeth his Idolles, meanyng couetouſneſſe in hys hert,
and commeth to hear gods word, doth therby prouoke
gods vengeaunce to hys vtter deſtruccion. Paule
ſayth and teſtifyeth that euery man whiche is circum-
cyſed, hath not profyt by Chriſte, is gone quite from
Chriſt, is fallen from grace. I ſaye and teſtyſye vnto
you in the word of the Lorde, yat ſo many of you as
be couetous, haue no profit by the preachyng of gods
word, the myniſtracion of hys ſacraments and the ſettyng
forth of pure religion wythin the realme: no ye be
clene from God framyng your ſelues vnto the faſſion of
thys worlde, ye can brynge forth no good frutes of
charitable workes nouriſhyng the rote of all euyll in
youre hartes, ye muſt nedes prouoke the wrath and
indignacion of god to your vtter deſtrucion, when as ye
kepe the ydoll of couetouſnes ſtyll in youre myndes to

[1] 1 Cor. iv. 1.   [2] Gal. iv. 19.

be honoured and ſerued in all your doinges, and yet pretend a zele and loue vnto the religion of Chryſt in your workes and ſayinges. I woulde fayne haue had iuſt occaſion to haue ſpoken at thys tyme ſuche thynges as myght haue bene confortable and pleaſaunt for you to heare.

But I muſte needes ſhewe the cauſes of gods wrath and indignacion kyndled agaynſte vs, leaſt that thoſe plages ſhould be aſcribed vnto the word and religion of Chryſt ſet foorthe amongeſt vs, whyche be procured by the wickednes of theym that ſeruyng couetous Mammon, haue forſaken, offended, and ſlaundered both Chriſt, and Chriſtes word and religion. No man can ſerue two maſters, whye then dooe ye pretend that ye be the ſeruauntes of Chryſt, ſeynge that ye wyll not forſake the ſeruyce of wycked Mammon? Yf ye be aſhamed to be named, and afrayd to continue the wycked ſeruauntes of wycked mammon, now ſhew and proue by youre ordinarye callyng, faythfull dealyng, and godly iudgement accordyng to thys example of Paule playnly paynted and ſet[teth] forthe in thys epiſtle vnto the Corinthians, that ye be Chriſtes mynyſters, the ſeruauntes and diſpoſers of gods myſteries and treaſures: for Paule ſhewing hym ſelfe as a good example of Chriſtes ſeruants, ſayth: *Sic nos æſtimet homo, ut miniſtros Chriſti. etc.*[1] So let a man eſteme vs, as the myniſters of Chryſt, and the dyſpoſers of the ſecretes of god. No man can come vnto Chriſte Ieſu to be hys myniſter, excepte he be drawen of the father. The father draweth not by force violentlye them that be ſtuborne and frowarde, but by loue them that be gentyll, and come wyllyngly. For when the father ſheweth in Chryſte forgeuenes of ſynnes, grace of amendement, iuſtificacion, and euerlaſtyng lyfe, then thoſe that make theim faſt theim ſelues wyth the bande of loue by deſyre of the ſame be drawen vnto Chryſt.

As contrary wyſe when the deuyll ſheweth in fleſhlye luſtes and worldly vanytyes, manye voluptuous pleaſures, then they that there wyth be entangled and

[1] 1 Cor. *iv.* 1.

delyted be drawen of the temptour away from Chryſt. Take hede therfore howe ye haue entred into religion, profeſſed chryſte, and receyued the goſpell. For if ye be drawen by loue of mercy, grace and ryghteouſnes, ye come vnto Chryſt: But by the deſyre of ryches, welth, and voluptuouſnes, men be drawen and tyſed away from Chriſte.

He therfore that by the profeſſion of Chriſt, the zele of hys worde, the fauoure of the goſpell, ſeeketh couetous gayne, or a carnal liberty, ſurely he is a ſeruaunt of Mammon, ennemy vnto Chriſte, and a ſclaunderer of the goſpel. For he that wyll be the ſeruaunt of Chryſte, muſt folow the example of Chriſt. He that wyll folowe Chriſt in example of lyuyng, he muſte forſake hymſelfe, take hys croſſe vpon hys backe dayly and folow Chriſt. So Chriſtes ſeruaunt ſhalbe deliuered from the bondage of ſynne, yat he may frely and wyllyngly contemnyng ye vanities of the world, and mortifying ye luſts of ye fleſh, ſerue chryſt in bearyng the croſſe of paynful diligence, to do the duty of his vocacion.

But all thoſe that delyte in a carnall libertye, or ſeeke vnlawfull geynes, althoughe they be named Chryſtians and fauourers of the goſpell, yet be they in dede not myniſters of Chriſt, but ennemyes vnto Chriſte: not louers of the Goſpell but ſclaunderers of the Goſpell, not iuſtyfied by liuelye faythe to be of that ryghteouſe ſorte for whoſe ſakes G O D ſpareth and fauoureth a common wealthe, but deceyued with a dead fayth to be of that vngodlye ſorte, for whoſe cauſe God plageth and deſtroyeth many a common welth. And nowe vndoutedly be we in great miſeries and daunger of deſtruccion, for that we haue many that be hearers, readers, and talkers of Gods worde, and fewe or none that do walke and lyue accordyng to gods worde: we ought truly to eſteme and take theym onlye to be myniſters of Chriſte whyche for the loue of mercy, grace, and ryghtuouſnes ſhewed of the father vnto theim in Chriſt do kyll the luſtes of theyr owne flefhe, dyfpyfe the vanytyes of the whole worlde, and forfakyng theyr own pleafures and commodities do take the croffe of paynfull diligence and walke after Chrift in doynge of theyr dutyes.

All other that haue the name and profeffion of Chryft without liuyng and conuerfacion accordynge therto, be fayned brethren, in feaftes wyth Chriften men to take parte of theyr good chere, vnclene fpots amongeft honeft company, feedyng theim felues without feare of god, clouds without any moifture of gods grace, toffed aboute wyth contrarye wyndes of ftraunge doctryne, trees paffyng fommer tyme without any frutes of good workes, twyfe dead without felynge the corrupcion of fynne, or lokynge to be graffed in the ftocke of grace, yea rooted vp from amongeft ye vynes of the Lord, wilde waues of the fea frothyng forth vnfhamefaft brags, and wandryng ftarres without conftancie in iudgement and opinion vnto whom the dungeon of darknes is ordeyned for euerlaftyng dampnacion.

What maruell is it then thoughe the vengeaunce of God be poured forth amongs them of fuch iniquitie, yea and moft abundantly when as hys word playnely preached, is of theym mofte wickedly abufed and fhamefully flandered, whych fay: Lorde, Lorde, and do not as they be commaunded of the Lord. Wherfore let vs fay: *Non nobis domine, non nobis*. Not vnto vs o Lord, not vnto vs, but vnto thy name geue glorye, not for that we by oure dedes haue deferued, but yat thy name O Chryfte amongeft vs chriftians may be honored, pardon our fauts, amende our liues, and indue vs with grace, that the lyghte of oure good workes afore men vpon the earthe, may caufe thee to be gloryfyed O Lorde in heauen. Dearlye beloued in Chrifte for the tender mercyes of god, when as ye fe carnall gofpellers, couetous ydolaters, greuyng youre confciences, flaunderynge Chriftes religion, and damnynge theyr owne foules, do not of malyce contempne difdayne and reuyle them, but of charitable pitye, lament, forow, and pray for theim, whyche blynded wyth ygnoraunce know not theim felues, deceyued wyth the deuyll, be drawen from Chrifte, comforte and faluacion, vnto euerlaftynge deathe and damnacion. Say and pray for them: O lorde fuffer not the enemye thus to lede into captiuitye owre felowes thy feruauntes, oure brethren thy chyldren, O Chryft reftore vnto lyberty them that you haft redemed wythe thy precious blud, fo yat we may altogether drawen of ye father, receyued of the fonne, and gided of the holy goft, be minifters of Chryft in libertye of the gofpell, delyuered from fynne frelye to delyte and take pleafure in a godly conuerfacion all the dayes of our lyfe. Nowe let vs after thys takynge of the mynifterye of Chryfte, w[h]yich perteineth generally vnto all chriftians, fpeake of the dyfpofers of Gods myfteryes, wherein we maye confider feuerally euery mans vocacion.

Paule dyd dyfpofe the fecretes of God by the preachynge of the Gofpell, whych was euer fecretly hydde from the wyttye, wyfe, and learned in the worlde. Other men in other vocacions muft dyfpofe other treafures of God by other meanes. As the magiftrate by authorytye muft dyfpofe the punyfhmente of vyce, and the mayntenaunce of vertue.

The rych man by liberalytye, muft dyfpofe reliefe and comforte vnto the poore and nedye. The Marchaunt by byinge and fellynge, and the craftes man by his occupacion, mufte prouyde vnto the common wealthe of neceffarye wares, fuffyciente plentye. The landelorde by lettyng of fermes muft dyfpofe vnto the tenants neceffary lands, and houfes of an indifferent rente. The houfbandmen by tyllyng of the ground and kepyng of cattel, muft dyfpofe vnto theyr landlordes, dew rentes, and vnto them felues and other. both corne, and other vytals. So euerye man by doynge of hys dutye mufte dyfpofe vnto other that commodytye and benefyte, whiche is committed of god vnto theym to be dyfpofed vnto other, by the faythful and diligent doyng of theyr dutyes.

The treafures of the Lord be vnmefurable, his hart is lyberall, ther can be therefore no lacke amonges hys people, yf hys ſtewardes vnto whom the dyſpoſing of hys gyftes be committed, be true and faythfull. Thys therfore faythe Paule, is requyred in a ſteward, yat he be faythfull. Who thynke ye, fayth Chriſt, is a faythefull and a wyſe ſtewarde whom the Lorde ſetteth ouer hys houſeholde to geue theim a due meaſure of the wheate of neceſſaryes in tyme conuenyente? Bleſſed is that feruaunte whom the Lorde when he commeth, ſhall fynde ſo doyng: verelye I ſaye vnto you that he wyl make him lord of all that euer he hath. Beholde the faythfulnes of the Lordes ſteward confyſteth in dylygente prouydynge and myniſtrynge vnto the Lordes famylye anye ſuche thynges as bee neceſſary. The reward of ſuch faythfulnes is to be put in truſt wyth all that his Lord and maſter hath. Then who can deſyre a better maſter then the Lorde God or a hygher roume then a ſtewardſhyppe in the houſe of Chriſt, or a greater reward then to haue all the treaſures of God whych be an hundred folde paſſynge any mans deſeruyng here, and furthermore euerlaſtyng lyfe. O that men wold conſyder the goodnes of God, the worthines of their offices, the comfortable felowſhyp of the houſhold of Chriſt, and the ioyfull rewarde of the croune of glory, and ſo be faythful ſtewardes and dyſpoſers of the manyfold gyftes of God: And not being bleared and blynded wyth couetouſneſſe, deſerue to be cut of from the company of chriſtians, and to haue theyr porcion with hypocrits, wheras ſhalbe waylyng and gnaſhing of teeth. For that ye gredy worme gnawyng the conſcience neuer dyeth, and the flamynge fyre of vntollerable vengeaunce ſhalbe neuer quenched.

O brethren, God hath geuen great plentye, and we in Englande fynde greate lacke: therfore the ſtuwards of God be vnfeythfull. Who be gods ſtewardes? They that haue gods gyftes. Suerly no man hath all the gyfts of God, and euery man hath ſome gyfts of God. Then if all thynges be lackyng, yet can no one man deſerue all the blame, but euery man ſhall be found fauty for that which is amyſſe, for lack of his duty.

Do ye perceyue that the laytie is eyther altogether ygnoraunte and blynd, or els hauyng knowledge to fpeake fayer, hath no learnynge to do well? Then fuerlye the cleargye hath not ben faythfull in preachyng of gods word earneftly, in fefon and out of feafon to reproue, befech and blame, in all pacience and token, or dyfcyplyne. Do ye fee the cleargye hath not wherwithall to mayntayne learnyng, to relieue the pore, to kepe hofpytalytye, and too fynde theym felues? Then trewly hath not the layitye fufficientlye prouyded that they whyche preache the Gofpell, fhould lyue on the Gofpell, and that they whyche fowe fpirituall treafures, myght repe corporall neceffaryes.

Do ye fee yat they which be in authoritye haue not ben regarded and obedientli ferued? Then ye common people haue not done theyr dutyes, dyfobeying any man placed in authoryty by gods ordynaunce. Do ye fe the people haue hadde iniuries and yet theyr complaintes neglygentlye heard and long delayed? then haue the higher powers omytted ryghteoufnes and iudgement, whiche wyl be required at theyr handes of the Lord.

Do ye fe that in all maner of thinges ther* is fome lack of that whyche is very neceffarye? Then be ye fure that all maner of men do leaue or myfufe fome parte of theyr dutye. *Quis poteft dicere: mundum eft cor meum, purus fum a peccato.*[1]

No manne canne fay: my hert is cleane, I am pure wythout fautes. Therefore feynge that we be all gyltye, Lette vs not enuye, grudge, or dyfdayne one an others faultes, but euery one acknowledge, lament, and mende hys owne fautes.

Do not triumphe and be glad when ye perceyue that other mens fautes be noted or rebuked, but be moofte certayne and fuer, that excepte ye fpedelye repente and amende, ye fhall euerye one be lykewyfe ferued. If ye haue not thofe fame faultes whyche ye heare by the preacher noted and rebuked, yet yf you take pleafure and be glad to heare other mens euyls, be fure

[1] Prov. xx. 9.

that euen that pleafure takyng is a faute, whyche God hateth and wyll punyſh.

Therefore when ye heare anye mannes fautes fpoken of, be forye for theim, and take hede to your felues: fo ſhall you thereby gette good and they haue no harme. If ye fo do at thys tyme, I may the more boldely examyne and trye the faythfulnes of fome ſtewardes and difpofers of Gods gyftes.

And for the better tryall and affurance[s] of theyr fydelytie I note two thynges to be requyred: fyrſte that a ſtewarde or difpofer be, *Quem conſtituit dominus*, whom the Lord affigneth and maketh: and fecondarily, *Vt det cibum in tempore*,[1] that he vfe to fede and cheryche, and not to deuoure and hurte theim of the lordes familye. For the fyrſte parte, it is to be noted, that euery man in the tyme of hys admyffion, when he ſhall be put into hys offyce, is fet on the hyll of confyderacion and aduyfement: where as the Lorde Chriſt to thofe whyche he admitteth, ſheweth that the harueſt is greate, the laborers be fewe, greate paynes muſte be taken that muche good may be done: vyle rebukes and greuous affliccions here to be fuffered, be the fygnes and tokens of great rewardes in heauen for theym prepared. The ennemy of Chriſt Satan vnto thofe whych he would deceyue ſheweth all the glory of the worlde, promyfyng to geue it a rewarde prefently vnto all them that wyl worſhyp hym fallyng downe at hys feete, in flattery, crafte, and iniquitye.

Chriſte the Lorde indueth wyth wyll and habilytye to take paynes to do good, thofe whych he bryngeth in at the dore to be ſhepherdes of the folde and ſtewardes of the houfe: the deuyll the ennemy of Chryſt cloketh [clothed] in ſhepe ſkynnes of folemne titles to gette gaynes, thofe whyche he conueyeth not in at the dore, but ouer an other waye to dyſtroye the flocke, and robbe the houfe.

Therfore yf thy roume be benefyce, prebende, offyce or authorytie in a chriſten comminaltye wythin Gods houfe, and yf thou be brought in at the doore of ordynarye and lawefull callynge, by paynefull dyligence to do good, thou mayeſt be a faythfull ſtewarde in that place:

[1] Luke *xii.* 42.

but yf thou be broughte in ouer and befydes all ordinarye and lawfull callynge, by couetous ambycyon to get gaynes, then muft thou nedes be a thefe and a robber: for Chryfte whyche fo fayth can be no lyer. I meane yf thou by money or fryndfhyp haue boughte eyther benefyce or offyce, thou canft not be of Chriftes inftitucion, but of the Dyuylles intrufion, not a fayethful dyfpofer, but a theuyfh extorcioner of Gods gyfts. For Chrift fayth playnely that he whyche entereth not in at the doore, but clymeth ouer an other way, is a thefe and a robber, and the thefe commeth not but to fteale, murther, and to deftroy.

The doore whyche is Chrifte hym felfe, can neuer be entred in at by eyther frendfhyp or money.

Sum perauenture wyl be offended not becaufe I fpeake againft the biinge of benefices, whyche be fpirituall charges, but for that I alfo include the bying and fellynge of offyces, whych as they faye, be temporall promocions. As for benefyces ye knowe fo well, that I neede net to ftand about the declaracion or profe in theym.

No, I am fure that ye perceyue howe that through the abufe of one benefyce, the Deuyll ofte tymes is fure to haue many foules.

Fyrfte the patron for hys prefentacion, then the Byfhoppe for admiffion, the perfon for hys vnworthyneffe, and a greate manye of the paryfhe that be loft for lacke of a good Perfons dutye.

But now as concernyng the biynge of offyces, to come thereby vnto the roume of an auditour, Suruciour, Chauncelloure, or anye fuche lyke, furelye no man wyll attempt it, but he whyche is fo couetoufe and ambycioufe that he dooeth neyther dread God nor loue man. Whereof commeth the byinge of offyces but of couetoufnes? howe then canne that be a good fruyte whyche fpryngeth oute of the roote of all euyll? Is not euerye Chryften common wealthe the folde of Chriftes fhepe, the houfe of hys famylye? be not then all offycers in a Chryften common wealthe named by Goddes woorde fheppeherdes of the fold, and ftewardes of the famylye of Chryſte? O Lorde what ſhall wee then ſaye to excuſe theim that by and ſel offyces wythyn England? Shall we ſay thoſe offyces be no roumes and places ordeyned of god for hys faythefull ſtewardes, therein to dyſpoſe hys treaſures and benefytes? or that the vile ſlaues of wycked Mammon for their brybery may lawfully be promoted vnto thoſe roumes whyche be ordeyned of God to hys holy ſeruauntes for theyr fydelytye? If we ſaye that the offyces be not meete for Gods ſeruauntes, then we confes that the offycers whyche be in theim be gods ennemyes. If we ſaye that they be ordeyned for the fayethfull ſeruauntes of god, how can we thynke that they maye be brought [bought] vnto the brybynge ſeruauntes of wycked mammon? Lette vs not ſeeke excuſes to cloke ſynne, no let euerye manne be knowen to be a lyer and ſpecyallye, they that ſay: One manne can ſerue twoo mayſters, Mammon in geuynge or takynge of brybes, and GOD in faythfull dooynge of duty. Let god be iuſtifyed when ye ſynde hys worde true, whyche plainly affyrmeth that they whyche clyme into a common offyce of Chryſtes fold by the help of Mammon in at the wyndowe of bryberye be theues and robbers, commyng to ſteal, murder and deſtroye.

O that no man in thys faute wer gilty, then myght I be ſure yat no man wold be offended. But and yf any man be greued becauſe hys ſore is touched, let hym remember the ſayinge of the wyſe man: *Meliora ſunt uulnera diligentis, quam fraudulenta oſcula odientis*:[1] the woundes of the louer be better then the deceytefull kyſſes of the hater. For the woundes whyche the frinde openeth, be to hele olde ſores; and the dyſceytfull kyſſes of the ennemyes be to make newe woundes. I ſpeake playnelye to open the wounde, to roote oute and heale the dyſeaſe of couetouſnes, whyche wold be to the wounded and to euery man, comfort. They that by flattery do couer, kyſſe, and playſter this deepe wounde, do ſeeke their owne gayne to the vtter dampnacyon of the wounded, and to good mennes greate griefe, yea and to the greate dyſquyetinge of a com-

[1] Prov. xxvii. 6.

mune welth: makynge no dyfference betwixt the Lordes feruauntes, and the Lords enemyes. For wythout dout, *Non est quem constituit dominus.*

He is none of the Lordes appoyntmente or admyssion, whyche entereth in to an offyce by brybyng, Monye, or flatterynge frendeshyp. Byinge of an offyce is an euydente token of vnfayethfulnes. He that is once knowen by that token and marke, shoulde be thrust out of the Lordes foulde, *Ne furetur, mactet, et perdat,*[1] leaste that he robbe, kyll, and destroye. But nowe by the seconde note to try whether that the steward and dyspofer of goddes treasures be faythfull or not, se whether that he be a feder or deuourer. He that fedeth, is fayethfull: he that deuoureth, is vnfaythefull. What doeth he whyche is vnfaythefull? deuoure goddes shepe, Christen people, the kynges subiectes; A daungerous matter, whiche if it be spoken of, wyl procure dyspleafure: and yf it be not remedyed, wyll procure Goddes vengeaunce. Surelye brethren, I thyncke God would neuer haue caused me to haue meddeled wyth thys daungerous matter, but that he wyll geue me grace more pacyentlye to suffer the losse of myne owne lyfe, then the damnacyon of your soules.

For yf I lose my lyfe here, I shall fynde it in heauen. But yf you be dampned, and I beynge a watcheman, and seinge your dampnacyon comming, do not geue warning, you shal be taken in youre owne synnes, and your bloude requyred at my hands. If I geue warnyng, and you take hede, gods indignacion shalbe appeased, and bothe we saued. Therefore I beynge a watcheman and by the lyghte of goddes worde spying that the abominacion of ydolatrous couetousnes hathe kyndled the indygnacyon of God to consume and destroye the people of thys realme, doo crye out agaynst Englande by the voyce of the Prophete: *Abiecerunt legem domini,*[2] they haue cast awaye the lawe of the lorde, euery one framyng hym selfe vnto the fashyon of thys world· *eloquium sancti Israell blasphemauerunt.*[2] They haue blasphemed the word of the holy one of Israell, by

---

[1] 1 John x. 10. [2] Isa. v. 24.

theyr abominable lyuyng. *Ideo incenſus eſt furor domini in populum ſuum:*[1] therefore is the indignacion of God kindled againſt his people. Therefore doth all runne at ſyxe and ſeuen, from euell vnto worſe: therefore doeth goddes worde take no place to do good, but is vnthankefully refuſed, whyche cauſeth more harm. Is gods word receyued in Englande becauſe it is playnlye preache and taughte, or refuſed and forſaken becauſe it is not obeyed and folowed? Be we in better caſe then we haue ben afore tyme becauſe papiſtry amongeſt vs is kept vnder, or els worſe then euer we were becauſe couetouſnes raygneth at lybertye? That whych papyſtry abuſed, hath not couetouſnes deſtroy[e]d? is not papiſtry ſuperſticion, and couetouſnes ydolatrye? Then I beſech you be not we well amended yat be come from abuſyng to deſtroying, from ſuperſticion to idolatry? And hath not God geuen vnto vs at the banyſhyng of ſuperſticion, comfortable plenty of his holy worde, and by the ſuppreſſyng of abbeyes excedynge aboundaunce of all maner of landes, ryches, and treaſures? And nowe where is it all become? Surelye it is muche ſpent, waſted and loſt by euyl officers, vnfaithful diſpoſers, whiche be in dede deuourers. Se therefore howe ye haue offended god, begyled the kyng, ſpoyled the realme, and indaungered your ſelues to be accuſed, condemned, and ſuffer as moſt vyle haynous traytours to God, the kyng, and to ye common welth. Wherfore whyles ye haue tyme, before ye be condemned, *Sacrificate ſacrificium iuſtitiæ, et ſperate in domino.*[2] Offer a ſacrifyce of ryghteouſnes, making reſtitucion of yat whych ye haue wrongfullye gotten: then truſte in the Lord, and he wyll ſhew mercy, prouydynge you pardon and ſafegarde, vnto euerye mannes comforte. Here I namynge no man, do meane almoſt euery man: for euery man hath ſome treaſures of the lords to dyſpoſe, and none is ſo faythfull that he maye be able to ſtande vnto the tryall, entryng wyth the Lorde into iudgemente. Therefore I aduertiſe both myniſters of the clergye, offycers in

[1] Isa. *v.* 25. [2] Ps. *iv.* 5.

authoritye, and other people of euerye degre, to acknowledge theyr faultes, and make reſtitucion to ye vttermoſt of theyr power. Firſt vnto the clergy, I ſay: there is none of you al hauing ſo much learninge, wytt, and dylygence, as is poſſyble to be in one man, that can do more then one mans duty: why then do ye take and keepe, ſome foure or fyue mens lyuynges? I do not thyncke that euery man is worthy blame that hath a great lyuynge, nor to be prayſed that hath a litle lyuyng. For as God hath geuen ſome more excellent gyftes of learnynge, wytte and polycy, ſo hathe he prouyded for the ſame better lyuynge with hygher authority: howbeit no man may promote hym ſelfe to procede from a meane lyuyng vnto a better, *quia nemo ſibi ſuimet honorem,* for no man may preferre hym ſelfe vnto honoure, *niſi qui a deo vocatus eſt,*[1] but he whyche for hys fydelytie in a lytle, is called of God to be truſted wyth more. But it is not a good reſon to ſay that becauſe an honeſt man for hys fydelyty is called of God from the leſſe vnto the more, therefore a couetous manne throughe gredynes, maye kepe leſſe and take more, and ſo ioyne thre or foure of theim together to make dyuers paryſhes in dyuers ſhyres, all one mans lyuynge. The Prophete cryeth: *uæ uobis qui coniungitis domum ad domum, et agrum agro copulatis.*[2] Wo be vnto you that yoine [ioyne] houſe to houſe and knyt fyeld vnto fylde. What reherſeth he no more but houſes and fyeldes? No, for ther was neuer ſuch abominacion in the prophetes times as to ioyne paryſhe to paryſh, prebend to benefyces, and Deanryes vnto knyghtes landes. I pray God that ſome of theim yf they be worthy men in wyſdome, learnynge and iudgemente, may be promoted vnto worthy roumes, and that thoſe meaner lyuynges whiche they haue heaped together to fyll one purſe, beynge ſo far dyſtante in place and condicions that they can neuer bee well ſerued of one mannes dutye, may be deuyded and dyſpoſed vnto meaner men: whych beyng more fitte for theſe lyuynges, maye do more good wyth theym.

[1] Heb. v. 4.   [2] Isa. v. 8.

I heare fome complayne and faye that all thynges bee nowe fo chargeable that one benefyce is not able to fynd one [an] honeſt man. And yf ye enquyre of the fame man whome they kepe and fynd in theyr benefyce they theim felues beyng abfent, they wyll fay a learned curate, and a dyligent farmer both honeſt menne. O wycked worldlings condemned by your owne words. The whole benefice yf you ſhuld therwyth be content ly[u]ing vpon it, and loke for no more, wolde not fynde one man.

But when ye haue gotten other promotions befydes that, to lye in another place from it, then a fmall porcyon of it doth ferue two honeſt menne whyche ye leaue in youre abfence. Herke you that haue three or foure benefyces. I wyll fay the beſt for you that can be fpoken: Thou lyeſt al wayes at one of thy benefyces, thou arte abfente alwayes from three of thy benefyces: thou kepeſt a good houfe at one of thy benefyces, thou kepeſt no houfe at three of thy benefyces, thou doeſt thy deutye at one of thy benefyces, thou doeſt no dutye at thre of thy benefices. Thou femeſt to be a good manne in one place, and in dede thou arte founde noughte in thre places. Wo be vntoo you worfe then Scrybes and Pharifeis Hypocrytes, whyche ſhut vp the kyngedome of heauen afore menne, kepynge the paryſhe fo that neyther you enter in your felfe, neyther fuffer them that would enter in and do theyr dewtye, to haue your roumes and commodities. Woo be vnte you dumme Dogges, choked wyth benefyces, fo that ye be not able to open your mouthes to barcke agaynſte pluralytyes, improperacions, bying of voufons, nor againſt anye euyll abufe of the cleargies lyuynges. No, for you* yowre felues myghte go a beggynge yf liuynges that be ordeyned for the cleargy wer not abufed, but reſtored and beſtowed vpon theym onelye that doeth the cleargyes dewtye. Therefore you be the inuenters and procurers of vngodlye ſtatutes, and deuelyſhe deuyfes, to gyue Lordes chaplaynes whyche oughte to lyue vpon theyr maſters wages, authorytye to lyue vpon the fpoyle of dyuers paryfhes. *Ad erubefcentiam ueſtram dico*,[1] I fpeake to make you afhamed of youre felues. If gentylmenne that be lordes feruauntes myghte obtayne of the kynge and hys counfel placardes or warrantes to kepe a ſtandyng vpon fhoters hyll, Salesbury playne, or in any theuyfhe place, to take mens purfes by the way, fhould not thys be robbery and fhamfull abhomination to be mayntayned by lawes, ſtatutes and authority? What fhold a yonge gentleman be afhamed to robbe one rych mans purfe of forty fhyllinges once in hys lyfe? and an auncient prelate not once blufhe whyche robbeth diuers pore paryfhes of forty pounds yerely al the dayes of hys lyfe. You peſtilent prelates whyche by flattery poyfon the hygh powers of authorytye, be ye neyther afrayed nor afhamed to make the Kynges maieſtye, his lawes and your lordes and maſters whych fhuld be the miniſters of iuſtice and equitye, to bee the defenders and mayneteyners of your vngodly robbery. Your eŝample and flattery hath caufed the great men and ryche men to take to theim felues the vauntage and profytes, and geue vnto their chyldren being ignoraunte babes, the names and tytles of Perfonnages, Prebendes, Archedeaconryes, and of all manner of offyces. For euen afwell may the Lorde that cannot, as the Doctoure that wyll not do his dutye, take the profites to hymfelf, and leaue a hyrelyng vnto the paryfh: and yet both be noughte. O that it woulde pleafe God to open the eyes of the hygher powers too perceyue what good doctryne, nay what deuylyfhe dyforder is taught by theim that be double and tryple benefyced. For theyr example teacheth, and theyre preachyng can neuer difwade, to fet and ordeyne ryche robbers and ignoraunt teachers ouer the Chryſten congregacion, goddes people, the kynges fubiectes: yea and as for cyuyll order in all offyces, ambicious couetous men learnyng at theim, take the folempne tytles and good fees vnto them felues, and leaue their dutyes vnto other, fo to be neglected and abufed, as

[1] 1 Cor. *vi.* 5.

cauſeth al diſcord and diſobedyence. For whoe but offycers ſhuld ſet good order, and make quietnes? And how can he ſet [ſee] any good order, whyche placeth hym ſelfe in ten mens roumes? or make other to be quyet wyth nothynge, that wyll neuer quyet hym ſelfe wyth any one liuynge? Yea how canne he be but a maker of buſynes yat thruſteth many menne oute of theyr lyuynges? But for all thys the flatterer wyl ſay that there is a great number of them that hath many mens lyuynges in theyr handes, whych do much good wyth them, yea and be liberall gentlemen, very good officers and godly preachers. But wotte ye what the ſcripture ſayth: they be *Canes impudentiſſimi, neſcientes ſaturitatem.*[1] Vnſhamefaſte dogges, knowynge no meaſure of gredye gettynge.

Derelinquentes rectam uiam errauerunt ſecuti uiam Baalam filii Boſor,[2] Leauyng the ryghte way of procedynge vnto greate fees by faythfull diligence in doynge worthye dutyes, do ſtraye in couetouſnes, folowyng Balaam the ſon of Boſor. Leauynge [Louyng] the rewarde of curſed in [and] wycked crafte, O take heede of Baalam you that loue the rewarde of iniquitye, a reward for curſyng the people, whome god would haue bleſſed. A fee for kepyng thoſe offyces vnto your ſelues whych god amongſt ye people wold haue executed. Can ye ſay any more for your ſelues then Balam dyd? *Si dederat mihi Balaac domum ſuam, plenam argenti et auri.*[3] If Balaac wold geue vnto me hys houſe full of ſyluer and gold, I cannot change the word of the lorde my God, to ſpeake more or les. Can ye do any better in the ſight of the world then Balaam did vpon the hylles, euen as the lord dyd commaunde hym and none otherwyſe? and yet louynge the reward of iniquitye beyng a Prophet, was rebuked of a bruyt beaſt: as you beyng wyſe men ought to learne at a folyſh Aſſe not to ouerburden and lode your ſelues with far more then ye ar able to beare. Suerlye it is an vngodly and wycked deſyre of you, to loke for a rewarde both of god for doyng* of* your* duty and alſo of Mammon for takynge vpon you farre more

---

[1] Iſa. *lvi.* 11.   [2] 2 Peter *ii.* 15   [3] Num. *xxii.* 18.

then euer ye be able for to dyfcharge. Balaam fought howe too get thanckes of God and a rewarde of Balaac, and in fo doyng he loft the fauoure of God, the rewarde of Balaac, and caufed the people too fynne, fo that the vengeaunce of God dydde fore plague the Ifraelites, and vtterly deftroyed Baalam and Balaac, and al theyr fort. And when as you by heapynge of lyuynges together, do feke to gette the welthe of the world, and alfo the fauour of god by pretendynge to do fo manye dutyes as no man is able to performe, ye lofe the fauor of god, and ye fhal be deceyued of the worlde, and bryng fuch iniquity amongeft ye people as fhall prouoke ye indignacion of god to plage theym, and to diftroy you. O for the tender mercies of god in oure fauioure Iefu Chrifte, although I rufhe and fret your legges vpon the hedge and pales of gods veneyarde, and fpeake playnely beinge but a very affe in comparyfon of your wyfdome, connynge, and experience, yet I befech you dere brethren be affured yat I fpeake not of malyce but of pyty, not of enuy, but of feare: for I fe euydently the aungell of the Lorde with a fworde of vengeaunce redye to deftroye you yf ye doo not ftaye, but procede in thys vngodlye way: Se and behold, *Nifi conuerfi fueritis, gladium fuum acuit, arcum fuum tetendit et parauit illum*,[1] excepte ye turne, he the Lorde hath whet his fword, he hath bente his bowe, and made it readye wyth deadlye dartes. Suerlye brethren this heapynge together of lyuynges maketh you to haue fo many thynges to do, that ye can do nothyng well: it is the readye waye not to edify but to deftroye. Wherefore yf ye cannot efpye your owne fautes in your felues, yet loke one at another: loke you of the layty at them of the cleargye, that feyng the motes in their eyes, ye may learne to pull the beames out of your owne eyes. Do ye not fe how that they of the cleargy by heapyng together manye lyuynges, haue caufed manye poore parifhes to pay their tithes yat lacke their perfons [Parfones]? Do ye not fe how that prebendes whiche were godly founded as mofte conuenient and neceffarye lyuyngs for

[1] Ps. *vii.* 12.

preachers to healp the byſhoppes and the perſons too enſtructe the people, be now vngodly abuſed to corrupte the byſhoppes and the perſonnes that rather ſeke the vauntage of good prebends to enryche them ſelues, then the healp of godly preache[r]s to enſtruct Gods people? Do ye not ſe howe theſe prouiders of pluralities hauynge the cure of Chriſten ſoules in the paryſhe, and ſhepefolde of Chryſt, do leaue the flocke and take the ſpoyle to ſpende in Noble mennes houſes, where as they doo ſe that the keper of horſes in the ſtable, of cattell in the fyelde, and of dogges in the kenell, doeth lyue on hys maſters wages, and not on the Pyllage of his cure. O ye noble menne do ye geue vnto the kepers of your horſes, cattell, and dogges, wages, leaſte that they ſhoulde ſell youre horſes, kyll youre cattell, or ſleye youre dogges to lyue vpon the ſkynnes: and wyl ye allowe your Chapleynes no wages, but cauſe theym to lyue vpon the murder and ſpoyle of the innocente Lambs of God, redemed and boughte wyth Chriſtes precious blode? Do ye ſe howe by theſe ſeruauntes of Mammon, enemyes of Chryſte, gredy wolues in Lamb ſkynnes, the paryſhes be ſpoyled, the people vntaughte, God vnknowen, hys lyuelye woorde ſette gracyouſlye forthe by the kynges procedynges, is vngracyouſly ſuſpected, hated, and abhorred of the ignorant people?

You of the laytye, when ye ſee theſe ſmall motes in the eyes of the clargye, take heede too the greate beames that be in your owne eyes. But alas I feare leaſt yat ye haue no eyes at all. For as hypocriſy and ſuperſtiticion dooeth bleare the eyes: So couetouſneſſe and ambycyon doeth putte the eyes cleane out. For yf ye were not ſtarke blynd ye would ſe and be aſhamed that where as fyfty tunne belyed Monckes geuen to glotony fylled theyr pawnches, kept vp theyr houſe and relyued the whol country round about them, ther one of your gredye guttes deuowrynge the whole houſe and makyng great pyllage throughoute the countrye, cannot be ſatiſſyed.

If ye had any eies, ye fhould fe and be afhamed to confeffe that yf fome of you fhoulde not haue manye offyces, there woulde not be menne ynoughe founde, to put in euerye offyce one manne, mete and able by doynge of theyr dewtyes to ferue the kynge, and take good order amongeft the people, where as there is a greate number too manye of your forte whyche thyncke your felues mete and worthye by takynge many Offyces in hande, to burden the kynge and the people wyth all fees and charges belongyng vnto euery offyce: yea and furdermore to requyre perfonages, prebendes, Deanryes and anye manner of lyuynge due vnto the Ecclefiaftycall miniftery, to be geuen vnto you for feruynge the Kynge in takynge the vauntage of many, and doyng the dutyes of fewe offyces belongyng vnto ciuyll pollycye.

If ye hadde anye eyes ye fhoulde fe and be afhamed that in the great aboundaunce of landes and goods taken from Abbeis, Colleges and Chauntryes for to ferue the kyng in all neceffaryes, and charges, efpecially in prouifion of relyefe for the pore, and for mayntenaunce of learnynge the kynge is fo dyfapoynted that bothe the pore be fpoyled, all mayntenance of learnyng decayed, and you only enryched. But for becaufe ye haue no eyes to fe wyth, I wyll declare that you may heare wyth youre eares, and fo perceyue and knowe, that were as God and the kynge hathe bene mofte liberall to gyue and beftowe, there you haue bene mofte vnfayethfull to dyfpofe and delyuer. For accordyng vnto gods word and the k[y]nges pleafure, the vniuerfities which be the fcholes of all godlynes and vertue, fhould haue bene nothyng decayed, but much increfed and amended by thys [the] reformacion of religion.

As concernynge goddes worde for the vpholdyng and increafe of ye vniuerfities, I am fure that no man knowyng learnyng and vertue doth doute. And as for the kynges pleafure it dyd well appeare in that he eftablyfhed vnto the vnyuerfityes all Priuileges graunted afore hys tyme, and alfo in all manner of paymentes requyred of the cleargye, as tythes, and fyrſt fruytes, the vnyuerſities be exemted. Yea and the kynges mayeſtye that dead is, dyd geue vnto the vniuerſities of Cambryge at one tyme, two hundred poundes yerely to the exibition and ſyndynge of fiue learned menne, to reade and teache dyuynitye, lawe, Phyſycke, Greke and Ebrue.

At an other tyme. xxx. pounde yerely *In liberam et puram elicmoſinam.* In fre and pure almes. And fynally for the fuſt dacion [foundation] of a newe Colledge ſo muche as ſhoulde ſerue to buylde it, and replenyſhe it wyth mo Scholers and better lyuynges then any other Colledge in the vniuerſitye afore that tyme had.

By the whyche euerye man maye perceyue that the kynge geuyng manye thynges and takynge nothinge from the vniuerſityes was very deſirous to haue them increaſed and amended. Howbeit all they that haue knowen the vnyuerſitye of Cambryge ſence that tyme that it dyd fyrſt begynne to receyue theſe greate and manyefolde benefytes from the kynges maieſtye, at youre handes, haue iuſte occaſion to ſuſpecte that you haue deceyued boeth the kynge and vniuerſitie, to en-ryche youre ſelues. For before that you did beginne to be the diſpoſers of the kinges liberalitye towardes learnyng and pouerty, there was in houſes belongynge vnto the vnyuerſytye of Cambryge, two hundred ſtudentes of dyuynytye, manye verye well learned: whyche bee nowe all clene gone, houſe and manne, young towarde ſcholers, and old fatherlye Doctors, not one of them lefte: one hundred alſo of an other ſorte that hauyng rych frendes or beyng benefyced men dyd lyue of theym ſelues in Oſtles [Oſtries] and Innes be eyther gon awaye, or elles fayne to crepe into Colleges, and put poore men from bare lyuynges. Thoſe bothe be all gone, and a ſmall number of poore godly dyly-gent ſtudentes nowe remaynynge only in Colleges be not able to tary and contynue theyr ſtudye in ye vniuerſitye for lacke of exibicion and healpe. There be dyuers ther whych ryſe dayly betwixte foure and fyue of the clocke in the mornynge, and from fyue vntyll ſyxe of the clocke, vſe common prayer wyth an exhortacion of gods worde in a commune chappell, and from ſixe vnto ten of the clocke vſe euer eyther pryuate ſtudy or commune lectures. At ten of the clocke they go to dynner, whereas they be contente wyth a penye pyece of byeſe amongeſt. iiii. hauyng a fewe porage made of the brothe of the ſame byeſe, wyth ſalte and otemell, and nothynge els.

After thys ſlender dinner they be either teachynge or learnynge vntyll v. of the clocke in the euenyng, when as they haue a ſupper not much better then theyr dyner. Immedyatelye after the whyche, they go eyther to reaſonyng in problemes or vnto ſome other ſtudye, vntyll it be nyne or tenne of the clocke, and there beyng wythout fyre are fayne to walk or runne vp and downe halfe an houre, to gette a heate on their feete whan they go to bed.

Theſe be menne not werye of theyr paynes, but very forye to leue theyr ſtudye: and ſure they be not able ſome of theym to contynue for lacke of neceſſarye exibicion and releſe. Theſe be the lyuyng ſayntes whyche ſerue god takyng greate paynes in abſtinence, ſtudye, laboure and dylygence, wyth watching and prayer. Wherfore as Paule, for the Sayntes and brethren at Hieruſalem, ſo I for your brethren and Saynctes at Cambrydge mooſte humblye beſeche you make youre colleccions amongeſt you rych Marchauntes of this citye, and ſend them your oblacions vnto the vnyuerſytye, ſo ſhall ye be ſure to pleaſe God, to comfort theim, and prouyde learned men to do muche good throughout all thys realme. Yea and truly ye be detters vnto theim: For they haue ſowen amongeſte you the ſpirituall treaſures of goddes worde, for the whyche they oughte to repe of you agayne corporall neceſſaries. But to returne vnto them that ſhoulde better haue prouyded for learnynge and pouertye in all places, but eſpecyally in the vniuerſities.

Loke whether that there was not a greate number of both lerned and pore that myght haue ben kepte, mayntayned, and relyeued in the vniuerfities: whych lackyng all healpe or comforte, were compelled to forfake the vniuerfitye, leue their bokes, and feke theyr lyuynge abrode in the country? Yea and in the cuntrey manye Grammer Scholes founded of a godly intent to brynge vp poore mennes fonnes in learnynge and vertue, nowe be taken aw[a]ye by reafon of the gredye couetoufnes of you that were put in truft by God, and the kynge to erecte and make grammer fcholes in manye places: And had neyther commaundement nor permiffion to take away the fcholmafters lyuyng in anye place, moreouer muche charitable almes was there in manye places yerely to be beftowed in pore townes and parifhes vpon goddes people, the kynges fubiectes: whiche almes to ye great dyfpleafure of god and dyshonoure of the kynge, yea and contrarye to goddes worde and the kynges lawes, ye haue taken away. I knowe what ye do faye and bragge in fome places: that ye haue doen as ye were commaunded wyth as muche charytye and lyberalitye towardes both pouertye and learnynge, as your commiffion woulde beare and fuffer.

Take heede whome ye flaunder, for Goddes worde, and the kynges lawes and ftatutes be open vnto euery mannes eyes, and be [by?] euery commiffion directed accordynge vnto them, ye both myght and fhould haue geuen much wher as ye haue taken much away.

Take hede vnto the kynges ftatutes, the actes of parliament, there ye fhall fynde that the Nobles and commons do geue, and the Kynge doth take into hys handes Abbeyes, Colleges and Chauntryes for erectynge of Gramer fcholes, the godly bryngyng vp of youthe, the farther augmentynge of the vnyuerfytyes, and better prouifyon for the poore. Thys fhall ye fynd in the Actes of parliament, in the Kynges ftatutes: but what fhalbe found in your practyfe and in your dedes? Surely the pullyng downe of gramer fcholes, the deuylifhe drownynge of youthe in ignoraunce, the vtter decaye of the vniuerſities, and mooſte vncharitable ſpoyle of prouyſion, that was made for the pore.

Was it not a godly and charitable prouyſion of the Kynge to geue vnto the vniuerſity two hundred poundes yerelye for excellente Readers? three hundred [Thirtie] poundes yerelye in pure almes, and manye hundred pounds alſo to the foundacyon and ereccion of a newe Colledge? And was it not a deuiliſhe deuyſe of you to tourne all thys the kinges bountuouſe liberalitye into improperacions of benefices, whyche be papyſticall and vncharytable ſpoyles of moſt neceſſarye prouyſion for pore paryſhes? *Intelligite inſipientes in populo, et ſtulti aliquando ſapite.*[1]

Learne vnderſtandyng you that playe vnwyſe partes amongeſte the people, and you fooles once waxe wyſe. *Qui plantauit aurem not audiet?*[1]

He that ſette the eares, ſhall he not heare the ſorowfull complaynte of pore paryſhes, agaynſte you that haue by improperacions clene taken awaye hoſpitalitye, and muche impared the due liuynges of gods mynyſters, the peoples inſtructoures and teachers. *Qui figurat oculum non conſiderat?*[1] he that faſhioned the eie, doth he not beholde howe that the beſte landes of abbeyes, colleges and chaunteries be in youre handes, and euyll improperacions conueyd to the kyng and to the vniuerſities and Byſhopes landes? *Qui corripit gentes non arguet?*[1]

He that corrected and punyſheth the heathen lackyng the lyght of gods word for the only abuſe of naturall reaſon, wyll he not reproue and condemne you whyche haue good reaſonable wyts, gods onely word, the kynges laws, and ſtatut[e]s: and much power and authority geuen vnto you to edifye and do good, ſeinge it is abuſed of you to deſtroy and do hurt? Shulde not you haue amended the prouiſion for the pore, the educacyon of youthe, and the condicion of the vniuerſities? And be they not by you ſore hurte and dekayed? The kynge ſhold and wold haue reformed religion. The fyrſt parte of reformacion is to reſtore

---

[1] Ps. xciv. 9, 10.

and geue agayne all fuche thynges as haue bene wrongfullye taken and abufed. Surelye the Abbeyes dyd wrongfullye take and abufe nothynge fo much as the improperacions of benefices. Nothynge is fo papyftycall as improperacions of benefices be: they be the Popes darlynges and paramors, whiche by the dyuelyfhe deuyce of wicked Balaamytes, be fet a brode in this realme to caufe the lerned men of the vnyuerfities and all bifhoppes that be godly menne, the Popes enemyes, to commyt fpirituall fornicacion wyth them. Whye dyd God deftroye the Madianytes but for their fynne? Why dyd he plage the Ifraelytes but for ye fame fynne? Why dyd God caufe the Abeyes to be deftroyed, but for papyftycall abufes? And why fhoulde not god plage the vnyuerfityes and Byfhops kepynge and meddelynge wyth improperacions, that bee the fame papyfticall and deuelyfh abufes?

O what a bloudye daye fhall it be: when as for thys abhomynacion, thys fpirituall fornicacion, God fhall commaunde hys faythfull feruaunte Moyfes the kynges mayefty to take and hange all the rulers of the people that haue wittynglye fuffred thefe whoryfhe Madyanytes, thefe Popyfh abufes? And caufe a zelous Phinees to fhedde the harte bloude of hym that before Moyfes and many Ifraelites, before a hygh iuftice and manye people, taketh a Madianite into hys tent, an improperacion into his enheritance. But nowe brethren as Peter preached vnto the Iewes: *Nunc fratres fcio quod per ignorantiam feciftis.*[1] Now brethren I knowe that you haue done thys through ignoraunce: for the Lorde whych forfeeth all thynges, knoweth that yf you hadde not bene blynded wyth ignoraunce, ye coulde neuer for pitye haue executed hys indignacyon and wrathe in makynge fuche deftruccyon. Seynge therefore that it was Goddes pleafure thus by one euyll to punyfhe an other, nowe repent, and amende, that youre fautes maye be pardoned. It pleafed God by the blynde malyce of the Iewes, to nayle Chryfte Iefu vpon the croffe: and yet as many of theim as hearyng that matter opened

[1] Acts *iii.* 17.

by Peter, were greued and pricted in confcience, fo many fayde vnto Peter, and to the other Apoftles what fhall we do? The Apoftolical counfel was: *Agite penitenciam, recipifcite.*[1] Repent and amend. So dere brethren hearynge and knowyng that God hath vfed your gredy couetoufnes to deftr[o]ye Abbeyes, Colleges, and chauntryes, and to plage all thys realme, be greued and fory in your hertes, feynge that ye haue bene *Vafa iræ,*[2] inftrumentes of wrath to execute vengeance: and purge your felues of thys vyle couetoufneffe, then fhall ye from henceforth be *Vafa honoris,*[3] veffels of honoure, to ferue God, *in fanctitate et iufticia*[4] in holynes and ryghteoufnes all the dayes of your lyfe.

And nowe on the other parte, you that be of the comynaltye, when ye feele that anye plague or punyfhement commeth by thiem that be fette ouer you in offyce, and aucthorytye, knowe that they do it not of theym felues, but be moued and ftyred of God, to worke hys wrath vpon you. For when as God was dyfpleafed wyth the Ifraelytes, then hys dyfplefure caufed Dauyd theyr kynge to take that way that brought a peftilence amongeft the people, whereon dyed. lxx. thoufande: *Addidit furor domini irafci contra Ifrael, commouitque dauid.*[5] The indignacion of the Lorde waxed whot agaynft Ifrael, and he ftired vp Dauyd. What kyndled the indignacion of God, but the fynnes of the people? The fynnes of the people dyd kyndle the indignacyon of the Lorde: the Lordes indignacyon ftired vp Dauyd in prefumpcyon. Dauids prefumptuoufnes caufed the people to dye on the peftylence. And euen as then God ordeyned yat chrift fhuld be crucifyed be ye malicious blyndnes of the Iewes, the Ifraelites plaged by the prefumption of Dauyd:

So hath he ordeyned that Englande fhoulde be fpoyled wyth gredy couetoufe officers, Looke then, what hath made thys greate fpoyle in England? gredye couetoufnes of officers. What dyd make in theym fuche gredy couetoufnes? the indignacion of God. What kyndled goddes indignacion? the fynnes of the

---

[1] Acts *ii.* 38; Mark *i.* 15.   [2] Rom. *ix.* 22.   [3] 2 Tim. *ii.* 21.
[4] Luke *i.* 75.   [5] 2 Sam. *xxiv.* 1.

people. What was the synne of the people? *Eloqui-um sancti Israell, blasphemauerunt.*[1] They haue blasphemed the holye woorde of GOD, callynge it newe learnynge and heretycall doctryne: *Ideo iratus est furor domini.*[1] And therefore is the wrath of the Lorde kyndled. Now you people which cry and say that you are robbed and spoyled of all that ye haue: Woulde ye haue thys whyche ye call robbyng and spoyling to be ceassed? Then quench the indignacion of god whych doth cause and make it. If ye wyl quench the indignacion of God, *Hodie si uocem eius audieritis.*[2] To daye, euen nowe yf ye shal heare hys voyce, harden not your hartes, as in the prouocacion in the daye of temptacyon. Harde heartes, styffe neckes, dysobediente myndes, prouoke, tempte, and styre vp the indignacion of God.

Truelye the indignacion of God shal neuer be quenched, vntyll that you wyth tender hartes, humble, obedyente, and thankefull myndes, receyue, embrace, and conforme your selues vnto the holy worde of God set forth by the Kynges Magestye his gracious procedynges.

There is as yet more styffe necked stubburnes, dieuellysh disobedience, and gredye couetousnes in one of you of the commune sorte that kepeth thys greate swellynge in the hearte, hauyng no occasion to sette it furth in exercise, then is in ten of the worst of theim that beynge in office and aucthoritye, haue manye occasions to open and shewe them selues what they be.

When dyd euer anye offycers in authorytye shewe suche rebellyous proud myndes, as was of late playnlye perceyued in very manye of the communaltye? I put the case that they be so couetouse, that one of their gredi guts had swalowed vp a whole Abbey, house, landes and goodes, And yf you had had powers vnto your wylles, ye had deuoured whole countryes, houses and goodes, men and beastes, corne and cattell, as ye dyd begynne.

Some of theim kepeth their fermes in theyr owne

[1] Isa. v. 24, 25.   [2] Ps. xcv. 7.

handes, and manye of you kepe youre owne Corne in youre owne barnes. Yea marrye, why fhould we not kepe oure corne in oure owne barnes? Forfooth ye nowe maye not keepe it for dreade of God, obedience to the Kynges maieftie, and pitie of your poore neighbours: For God fayeth: *Qui abfcondit frumenta, maledicetur in populis: benedictio autem fuper caput uendencium:*[1] He that hydeth vp corne, fhall be accurfed amongeft [amonges] the people: but bleffynge fhal be vpon theyr heades that bryngeth it furth to the Markettes to fell. Here ye heare the bleffynge and curfe of God.

Ye knowe the kynges gracious Proclamacyon, ye maye perceyue youre neyghbours neede, by theyr myferable complaynt. And yet neyther God by bleffyng and curfynge, neither the kyng by proclamacion and commiffion, nether the pore by praiyng and paying can caufe you to ferue ye Markets wyth corne. But let goddes woorde, the Kynges lawes, honeft order, and charytable prouyfyon be put foorth of all markette townes by wycked Mammon, and let hym onely kepe the Markets and fet pryfes for youre purpofes, and wythoute doubte euerye market fhalbe ful of all manner of Corne and vytayles commyng in on al fydes.

O wycked feruauntes of Mammon, alwayes bothe ennemyes and traytoures to G O D and the kyng and the common wealthe. Is it God or Mammon that hath made the Corne to fprynge, and geuen you plentye? Yf ye fay Mammon, then ye confeffe playnely whofe feruauntes ye be, what Idolatrye ye vfe. If ye fay God, How dare ye confeffe him in youre woordes and denye hym in youre deedes? Whye do ye not brynge foorth goddes corne vnto goddes people, at goddes commaundement? Why be ye not faythfull difpofers of Goddes treafures? Well, he yat hath no corn thinketh he hath no parte, nor is not gyltye in this matter: but I can tel that ther is many of theim, that neither hath nor wyll haue corne, whyche make corne moft dere. I haue heard howe that euen this laft yere, ther was certayn Acres of corne growyng on the ground

[1] Prov. xi. 26.

bought for. viii. poundes: he that bought it for. viii. fold it for. x. He that gaue. x. pounds, fold it to an other aboue. xii. poundes: and at laſt, he that caryed it of the ground, payde. xiiii. poundes. Lykewyſe I hearde, that certayne quarters of malte were boughte after the pryce of. iii. ſhyllynges. iiii. pence a quarter to be delyuered in a certayn markette towne vpon a certayne daye. Thys bargayne was ſo oft bought and folde before the daye of delyueraunce came, that the ſame Malte was folde to hym that ſhoulde receyue it there and carrye it awaye, after. vi. s. a quarter. Looke and ſe howe muche a craftes man or anye other honeſte man that muſte ſpend corne in his houſe, by this maner of bargaynynge, payeth, and howe littel the houſbande manne that tylleth the ground, and paieth the rent, receyueth: Then ye may ſe and perceyue it muſt needes be harde for eyther of theim to kepe a houſe, the cra[f]tes man payinge ſo muche, and the huſbandman takynge ſo lytle.

There is a lyke maner of barganyng of them that be leaſemongers, for leaſemongers make the tenaunts to pay ſo muche, and the landlord to take ſo little, that neither of them is wel able to kepe houſe. I heare ſay that within a few miles of London an honeſt gentleman did let his ground by leaſe vnto pore honeſt men after. ii. s. iiii. d. an acar: then commeth a leſemounger, a theſe, an extorcioner, deceiuyng ye tenaunts, bieth theyr leaſes, put theim from the groundes, and cauſeth them yat haue it at hym nowe, to paye after. ix. s. or as I harde ſaye. xix. s. but I am aſhamed to name ſo muche. How be it, couetous extorcioners be aſhamed of no dede be it neuer ſo euyll. And as I hear ſay, ther be many leſemongers in London, that heyghthen the rent of bare houſes: and as corne, landes, tenementes and houſes, ſo in al maner of wares, ther be ſuch biers and ſellers as cauſe ye prouyders and makers of ye wares to take ſo litle, and the occupiers of the wares too paye ſo muche, that neyther of theim both is able too lyue. All the Marchauntes of myſchyefe that go betwixt the barke and the tree. Betwixte the houſband man that getteth the corne, and houſholder that occupyeth Corne, betwix the Landlorde, that letteth fermes, and the tennauntes that dwell in the fermes. And betwixt the craftes man that maketh, or the marchaunte that prouydeth wares, and other men that occupieth wares. I ſaye theſe marchauntes of miſchiefe commynge betwixte the barke and the tree, do make all thinges dere to the byers: and yet wonderfull vyle and of ſmall pryce to many, that muſt nedes ſett or ſell that whyche is their owne honeſtlye come bye. Theſe be far worſe than anye other that hath bene mencyoned heretofore: for although benefyced men and offycers haue manye mennes liuynges, yet they do ſome mennes dutyes. But theſe haue euerye mannes lyuyng, and doo no mans duytye. For they haue that whyche is in dede the lyuynge of craftes men, Marchauntmenne, huſbandmen, landelordes and tennauntes, and do neuer a one of theſe mens dutyes. Theſe be ydle vacaboundes, lyuyng vpon other mens labours: theſe be named honeſt barginers, and be in dede craftye couetouſe extorcioners. For they that be true marchauntemen to by and ſell in dede, ſhoulde and doo prouyde great plentye and good chepe by honeſt byenge and ſellynge of theyr wares. But theſe hauynge the names of true marchauntes, and beyng in dede crafty theues, do make a ſcarſitye and dearth of all thynges that commeth through theyr handes.

Take awaye all marchauntmen from anye towne or cytye, and ye ſhall leaue almoſt no prouyſyon of thinges that be neceſſarye. Take awaye leaſmongers, regrators and all ſuche as by byinge and ſellynge make thyngs more dere, and when they be gone, all thyngs wylbe more plentye and better chepe. Now maye ye ſe who they be that make a greate dearth in a great plentye. For who is it, that heygtheneth the pryce of Corne, the houſbandman that getteth plentye of corne by tyllynge of the grounde? No: the regrator that byeth corne to make it dere, growynge vpon the grownde. Who reyſeth the rentes, ioyneth houſe to houſe, and heapeth fermes together? The Gentyll manne, that by geuynge of leaſes, letteth forth hys own landes into other mennes handes? No, the leaſemongers, that by felling leaſes, byeth and bryngeth other mennes Landes into their own hands. Who maketh all manner of wares and marchandyſes to be very dere? the marchaunt venterer, which with fayethfull dylygence to prouyde for the commune wealth, caryeth furth ſuche thynges as maye well be ſpared, and bryngeth home ſuche wares as muſte needes be occupyed in thys realme? No, the Marchant of myſchyeſe that by craftye conueyaunce for his owne gayne, caryeth awaye ſuch thinges as maye not be ſpared, and bryngeth agayne ſuche wares as are not nedefull. Take hede you Marchauntes of London that ye be not Marchauntes of myſchyeſe, conueying away to much old lead, wol, lether and ſuch ſubſtanciall wares as wold ſet many Englyſhmen to work, and do euery manne good ſeruyce, and bryngynge home fylkes and ſables, cattayls, and folyſhe fethers to fil the realm full of ſuch baggage as wyll neuer do ryche or poore good, and neceſſary ſeruyce. Be ye ſure, if thys realme be rych, ye ſhall not nede to be poore, yf thys realme be poore, you ſhall not be able to kepe and enioy your ryches. Take hede than that your marchaundiſe be not a ſeruynge of folyſh mens ſanſies, whyche wyll deſtroye the realme: but lette it be a prouydyng for honeſt diſcrete mens commodities, whych wyll be the vpholdyng and enrychyng of you and the whole realme. Take hede vnto your vocacions prelates and preachers Magyſtrats and offycers, landlordes and tenaunts, craftes men and marchauntes, all maner of men take hede vnto youre ſelues and to your conuerſacion and lyuyng: yea dere brethren at the reuerence of god, for a generall comfort to al partes with out gredye couetouſneſſe towards oure ſelues, or malicious enuye towardes other, wyth a ſyngle eye, of a pure herte, let vs conſyder and acknowledge how that the bountifull liberalitye of almyghtye God hath geuen vnto thys realme wonderfull plenty of perfonnages, prebends, benefyces, offyces, and all maner of lyuynges: wyth great aboundance of corne, cattell, landes, goodes, and all wares that be good and profitable: and howe that it is certeynly the vnfaithfull difpofers whyche caufe a great fcarfyty, dearth and lacke of all thefe giftes and treafures of God, therfore *dominus de cælo profpexit, ut uideat fi eft intelligens aut requirens deum.*[1]

The Lord loked doun from heauen to fe yf there were any that had vnderftandyng and fought to pleafe God in faythfull dyfpofynge of Goddes treafures: but feinge that *Omnes ftudent auaritiæ, a maiore vfque ad minorem.*[2] All be geuen vnto coueteoufnes from the hyefte vnto the lowefte, fo that pore people can haue no houfes to dwell in, ground to occupye, no nor corne for their moneye. The Lorde hym felfe fpeakyng vnto the earthe, fheweth wher is the faute: *principes tui infideles.*[3] Thy head rulers and offycers be vnfaythfull difpofers. *Socii furum,*[3] theuifhe fellowes.

Omnes diligunt munera,[3] they all loue brybes, *et fequuntur retributiones,*[3] and hunte for promocyons. What then O Lorde fhall be the ende of all thys? *Viuo ego dicit dominus.*[4] As trulye as I lyue fayeth the Lord *propterea quod facti funt greges mei in rapinam,*[4] Becaufe that my flock haue ben fpoyled, *et oues meæ in deuorationem omnium beftiarum agri,*[4] and my fhepe deuoured of all wyld beaftes of the fyelde, *quia non effet paftor,* Becaufe there was no keper, *Neque enim quæfiuerunt paftores mei gregem meum,* For thofe [thefe] which were named my paftours, dyd take no heede vnto my flocke, *Sed paftores pafcebant femetipfos,* But thofe paftours dyd feede theym felues prowlyng for profyte, *et greges meos non pafcebant,* and my flocke th[e]y dyd not feede by dooyng of their dutyes. *Propterea paftores audite uerbum domini.*

Therfore ye keepers heare the word of the Lorde. What worde? that the flocke fhalbe delyuered, and you fhalbe deftroyed: That is a true word: for *qua menfura*

[1] Ps. *liii.* 2.   [2] Jer. *vi.* 13.   [3] Isa. *i.* 23.   [4] Ezek. *xxxiv.* 8, 9.

mensi fueritis, remecietur uobis:[1] By [bicause] the same
measure that you haue serued other, ye youre selues shall
also be serued: for as ye haue serued superstycious
papistes, so shall you your selues be serued, beynge couetous Idolaters: yea and haue as muche vauntage at the
metynge, as is betwixte supersticion and Idolatrye.
Howe be it, God geuynge you respite to loke for amendmente: offers more gentelnes, yf ye wyl take it. For in
the. xx. of Ieremy he sayth: *Ecce ego do coram uobis uiam
uitæ et uiam mortis:*[2] Behold I set before you the way of
lyfe and the way of death: yf ye repent and amend,
lyfe: If ye be styll stifnecked, death: for the Lorde by
Esaye. i. sayeth: *Si uolueritis et audieritis:*[3] Yf ye wyll
heare to repent and amend, *Bona terræ comedetis,*[3] ye
shall eat the good fruits yat the earth shall brynge
forth, to your comfort. *Si nolueritis, et me ad iracundiam prouocaueritis,*[3] yf ye wyl not, but prouoke me
to anger, *gladius deuorabit uos.*[3] The sworde shall eate
you vp. *Quia os domini locutum est.*[3] For it is Gods
owne mouthe that hathe spoken it. For Gods sake
beleue it: And do not by an harde hearte voyde of
repentance heape vnto your selues the wrathe of god
agaynst ye day of vengeance.

But thankfullye enbrasynge the ryches of goddes
goodnes, pacience and long sufferyng, acknowlegyng
that goddes kyndnes draweth you vnto repentance, yf
ye haue so lytle spyrituall felyng and ghostlye vnderstandynge that ye can nothyng be perswaded or moued
by the comfortable promyses, and terrible threatenynges of the inuisible God: yet hauynge corporall eyes
and naturall reason, consyder the decaye of thys
Realme, and the towardnes of the kynges magestye.
Note the decaye of thys realme, and thereby ye shall
learne to knowe that nothynge can make a realme
wealthye, yf the inhabitauntes therof be couetouse: for
yf [all] landes and goodes coulde haue made a realme
happy notwythstandynge mennes couetousnes, then
shoulde not thys realme soo vnhappylye haue decayed,
when as by the suppression of Abbeis, Colleges and Chaunteries, innumerable lands and goodes were gotten.

[1] Matt. vii. 2. [2] Jer. xvi. 3. [3] Isa i. 19, 20.

If goddes worde were ordeyned by anye other meane then by the conuertynge of couetous men, to make that realme happy where couetous men be, then fuerlye fhoulde England now be moft happy, wher gods word is frely fet forth in the mother toung, playnly preached in folempne congregacions, and commonly vfed in daily communicacion. But vndoubtedlye whereas couetoufe men be, there neyther landes or goodes, no not goddes holye Gofpell canne doo fo muche good as couetoufnes doeth harme. Wherefore feyng thys realm by couetoufneffe is foore decayed, leaft it fhoulde alfo by the fame be deftroyed, awaye wyth youre couetoufnes, all you yat loue thys realme. Or yf ye wyll not do it for loue of the realme, yet for the reuerente obedience whyche ye owe vnto God and the kynges maieftie, away wyth couetoufnes whyche maketh men feruauntes of Mammon, and enemyes vnto god and the kynge. Be ye well affured that the kynges Maieftye whyche nowe is, God faue his noble grace, dreadeth god, loueth his people, and abhorreth couetoufnes, whiche in this realme offendeth God, difhonoureth ye kyng, anoyeth the people.

Therefore he doeth partly nowe perceyue and confider, and wyll do better hereafter, that prelates wyth pluralities, and magyftrates wyth manie offices, do burden him and his people wyth paying tithes, fees, and manye greate charges, and yet kepe fo many roumes vacant of prechers and officers, that his magefty cannot be duly ferued, nor his people well inftructed by the preachyng of gods word, nor yet well ordred by the myniftracion of iuftice and equitye.

He knoweth that regratours of corne vyttals and of all maner of wares, make fuche dearthe and fcarcitie, that no diligence of good marchauntes by honeft byinge and fellynge canne prouyde anye thynges to be eyther good cheap or plentiful. It is well knowen to his gracious maiefty, or at the leaft vnto hys honourable councell that leafemungers takynge muche of tenauntes and paying lyttell vnto the landlordes, haue both they

lyuynges, and doth the dutyes of neyther. For to
theyr owne pryuate luker they take rentes of tenauntes,
and fermes of landlordes: but when by occafyon they
fhall be requyred to ferue the Kynge for a common
wealth, then they wyll haue neyther landes nor ferme
to do the kyng feruyce. Do not therfore imagyn you
that be eyther of the clergye or of the laytye in hyghe
or lowe degree, that the Kynges Gracious Mageftie
and his honourable councell be fo negligent that they
do not efpye, or fo parcyall that they wyll not punyfhe
thofe whyche in thys realme hynder the prechyng
of gods word, ftoppe the adminyftracion of iuftice
and equitye, caufe of all thynges a dearthe and fcarfytye, and brynge Gentlemenne to poouertye, and huf-
bandmen vnto beggerye. It is fpyed and mufte be
punyfhed, although it be delayed for a tyme, to fe yf
you of your felues wyllynglye wyll amende it.

Beware therefore that ye ftaye not your felfe vnto a
bryttell ftaffe, for it wyll braft in fpylles and perce
thorowe your handes. Do not ftay your felfe vpon
thys ymaginacion to thynke that althoughe craftelye
contrary to lawe and confcience ye do inuade other
mennes roumes, liuynges and goodes, yet for becaufe
ye be fo many in number that do it, therefore the
kynge and hys councell eyther cannot or wyll not bee
agaynfte you in it: For trulye euen therefore mufte
they nowe neades wythout delaye reforme and amend
it. For as fedicious rebellion, fo couetoufe treafon
beynge in a fewe may be fuffered at the fyrfte in hope
of amendment, fo long as they few by clokynge it
fecretelye, feme to be afhamed of their owne euyll
doynges, or afrayed of the rulers power and authorytye:
but beynge fo many that they all together wythoute
fhame and feare, falle to open fpoylynge of the realme,
then wythoute delaye mufte they needes be repreffed,
althoughe they both fay and fweare, that they be the
kyngs fubiects, and breake no laws. If ye fpoyle be
found in theyr hands, it is neyther fayinge nor fwear-
ynge that can excufe them. Open fpoile hath bene

made of perfonages, prebendes, offices, fermes, wares, vyctuals, and of all manner of mens liuinges. Therefore there is no long delay to be taken in hope of amendemente, but fpedye prouifion for redres muft be made for feare of a generall deftruccion. You then that for waftynge and abufynge of the Lordes goodes be worthye and lykely fone to be difplaced, yet in ye mean tyme whyles ye haue refpyte, playe the parte of a wyfe fteward. Reftore vnto preachers and offycers, benefyces and offyces: lette landelordes haue their rentes, and fermoures theyr leafes: caufe byinge and fellyng to be a prouyfyon of good chepe and plentye, and not an occafyon of dearthe and fcarfytye. Soo fhall both God and the kyng perceyuyng your wyfe prouyfion, allow your wel doyng, pardon your fautes, and confirme you in your offyces.

O refufe the feruyce, reftore the iniuryes of wycked Mammon, that ye maye from hencefoorthe feruc God and the kynge, prouydyng for the people in holynes and ryghtoufnes all the dayes of youre lyfe: take hede when ye go from a meaner lyuynge vnto a better, frome a lower offyce vnto a hygher, that ye goo as menne called of Chrifte, not as bewitched and allured by Mammon, fe that God by hygher authoritye perceyuynge your faythfulnes in a lyttell, doo in at the doore of worthynes and honeftye, admytte and receyue you to be trufted wyth more: beware leafte that the deuyll by flatteryng frendfhyppe and couetous ambycion, perceyuynge your worldlynes in a lytle, do in at the wyndow of wycked bryberye conuey and receyue you, to abufe and be abufed wyth more. Se that ye obey the commaundement of God, takynge paynes in youre dutye to feede and doo good. Do not confent vnto the temptacion of the Deuell, worfhyppynge hym in worldlynes, for to gette gaynes. Thefe thynges obferued, ye fhal be eftemed and taken as worthye minyfters of Chryft, and feruaunts of God, for fo much as appertayneth vnto the lawfull callyng and admiffion of you into youre rowmes, and alfo the fayethfull dylygence in vſyng of your ſelues in your roumes. Furthermore Paule geueth example of a lowly mynde whyche doeth not iuſtifye a mans ſelfe, and iudge euyll of other. For ſo it becommeth the ſeruauntes of God, and the mynyſters of Chryſte, euen when they haue done as they be commaunded, to acknowledge them ſelues vnproſytable ſeruaunts. And not as proud Phariſeis, prayinge in the preſence of the Lorde, to make boaſt of theim ſelues, and fynde fautes wyth other men. No, for yf other menne prayſe them, they muſt not regarde it, no nor yf theyr owne conſcience commende them, excepte God alſo allow it. Therfore Paule ſayeth. *Mihi pro minimo eſt ut a nobis iudicer.* It is one of the leaſt thinges wyth me too be iudged of you that be wyth me, eyther in tyme or place. *Vel ab humano die,* eyther of mannes daye, by the experience of theim that ſhall haue further tryall in contynuance of tyme. *Sed neque me ipſum iudico.* No nor I doo not iudge my ſelfe. *Mihi enim nihil conſcius ſum, ſed non ideo iuſtificatus ſum.* For there is nothyng that I knowe my ſelfe gylty of, yet through that am I not iuſtifyed, no not thorow the iudgement of you or of other, or of myne owne conſcience. *Qui uero iudicat me dominus eſt.*[1] He truly yat iudgeth me, is ye lord iudge of all men. *Quare, nihil ante tempus iudicate,*[1] wherefore iudge ye nothyng afore the tyme of iudgemente. *Quando dominus uenerit,*[1] when the Lorde ſhall come to iudge. *Qui et illuſtrabit occulta tenebrarum,*[1] whyche alſo ſhall make bryghte the couertes of darkeneſſe and craftye clokynge of fautes. *Et manifeſtabit concilia cordis,*[1] and ſhall open the thoughtes of the heartes, whiche he only ſearcheth. *Et tunc laus erit unicuique a deo.*[1] And then prayſe ſhall be vnto euery one of God, that geueth prayſe to the prayſe worthy. If Paule, beynge a mynyſter of Chryſte, and a diſpoſer of Goddes myſteryes, was ſo faythefull in hys doynge that neyther all the worlde nor hys owne conſcience coulde in any thyng reproue hym, and yet to contynue hys carefull dylygence had euermore a greate reſpecte vnto the commyng and

[1] 1 Cor. *iv.* 3, 4, 5.

iudgement of the Lorde: Howe fhall we thynke that they rede and take thys place, whiche beyng knowen both to theym felues and vnto the whole worlde to do very euyl in many thynges, yet wythout care of amendement, do forget theym felues, the Lord, and his iudgemente? Surely they vnderftand it as Peter fayth: that many places of Paul be vnderftand of them whych beyng *inducti* καὶ ἀστήσιχτοί vnlearned and vnfetled in iudgement, ασριβλοναει wraft or wryng vntyll a wrong pin *in fuam ipforium pernicicm*,[1] vnto theyr owne deftruccyon, manye places of Paule, *et reliquas fcripturas*,[1] and the other fcriptures. For whereas thys place of Paul fhould be applyed to make men carefull and diligent, they wraft and wryng it to make for them that be careles and negligent. For Paul fayth that he doth very lytle regarde what any man doth iudge of hym, menyng therby that though all the world wolde commende hym, yet wold he not be vayne glorious, of hys well doynge. They faye, they paffe lytle what any man faythe by them, meanyng therby that though all men fynde fautes wyth theim, yet wyll they neuer be afhamed of theyr euyll doynge. Paule fayeth that no man fhoulde iudge, meanynge that no man as concernynge fecretes of the mynde, fhould iudge other to be yuell, and theim felfes to be iuft: and fo take occafion to fpeake fhamefully of other, and to glory in theim felues: they faye that no man fhoulde iudge, meanynge that neyther preacher nor friende fhoulde fo rebuke theyr manifeft euyll dedes, as myght geue theym occafion to be afhamed of theym felues, and leue iudgynge of other. Lette vs not wreft the places of Paule and of other fcripturs vnto a wrong purpofe. They wreft the faying of Paule vnto a wrong meanynge, when as the mercye of God, whyche paffeth all hys works is denyed of theym vnto anye penytente fynner, by theyr allegynge of the tenth of Paul vnto the Ebrues. Then is that place not well applied but wrong wrefted. For when it is fayde that yf we fynne wylfullye after that we haue receiued the knoweledge of the trueth, there

---

[1] II. Peter *iii.* 16.

remayneth no more sacrifice for synne, but a fearefull lookynge for iudgemente and violente fyer, it is a meante that there is remaynynge and leaste in the scriptures no mencyon of sacrifyce for the forgeuenesse of synnes, but terrible threatnynges of vengeaunce to punyshe synners, too bee preached vnto wylfull synners.

Howbeit there is no condemnacion but alwayes mercye to be preached vnto theym that grafted in Christ Iesu, be penitent synners, how sore and ofte soeuer they fall. For his mercy is aboue all hys workes. Therefore whensoeuer he suffereth the Deuyll to tempte menne to do synne, or too plage them for synne, or whensoeuer by his worde wrytten or preached he doth aggrauate synne, all is done to dryue menne vnto mercye. The deuyll hathe caused here in Englande muche synne and abhominacion, greuous plages, and sore miseries, God hath sent wonderous plenty of hys confortable word. And nowe brethren all this is euen the worke of god: for it is God that worketh al thynges in all men. *Deus est qui operatur omnia in omnibus.*[1] And yet take good hede to the true interpretacion of thys place least that ye make God to be the author of syn, *Qui non nouii peccatum, nec est inuentus dolus in ore eius.*[2] whyche knoweth no synne by experience of doyng it, nor hathe no gyle founde in hys mouthe. But euen as it was God that dyd both geue and take awaye Iobs goodes: So is it God that doth al thyngs, both good and euyll. And as he dyd make Iob ryche, by geuinge him goodes, and poore bi suffering [and vsyng] the deuill to destroy those goodes: so doethe he good deedes of hys owne goodnes, and euyll dedes in sufferynge the deuyll to do theym. Yea it is euen God that hathe concluded al men under synne, that hath suffered the deuyl to tempt al men* to do synne, yea and *scriptura conclusit omnia sub peccato,*[3] ye scriptur of God hath concluded al men vnder syn, or as Paule speaketh in an other place more pla[i]nli αιτοάμεθα. We haue concluded or proued, allegynge good reason, that both the grekes and the Iewes be vnder synne. So nowe

[1] 1 Cor. *xii.* 6   [2] 1 Peter *ii.* 22.   [3] Gal. *iii.* 22.

all ye by G O D be concluded vnderneth finne, that is
by goddes fuffraunce the deuil hath caufed you to commit finne. By Gods ordinaunce the fcriptures and the
preachers of God, do open and declare that ye be all
fynners. And this is all done, *ut omnium miferearetur*,[1]
that he myght haue mercye vpon all, that all mighte
receyue the pardon of his mercye without ye which
none can be faued, none can efcape vengeaunce.
For *non eft in aliquo alio falus*, there is no health in
anye other, *nec aliud nomen datum fub Cælo, in quo
oporteat nos faluos fieri*,[2] nor none other name geuen
vnder heauen, in the which we fhuld be faued. So
yat he whyche wyl haue anye healthe mufte come vnto
Chrift, fhewyng him felfe wounded with fin, to ftand in
nede of Phificion. He yat wil be faued muft fhew him
felfe a penytente fynner vnto Chrifte which came not
to cal the righteous but fynners to amendmente. But
he yat regardeth the flattery of the worlde or the parci-
alitie of his owne confcience, and therby taketh occafion
to glory in his own doynges, he fhal finde no mercy, he
can receiue no pardon or forgeuenes fent from god to
be deliuered only vnto thofe yat fele and acknowlege
them felues to be fickely and vnrighteous finners.
Thei therfore that fele and acknowledge ye greateft fins
wickednes* and abhominacions in theim felues being
fory therfore, and entend amendment, be moft worthi
and fure to receiue ye great pardon of gods mercy,
whyche certenly wil deliuer them out of all daunger,
kepe them in fafti and bryng them to profperity.
Heare therfore and I wil now read my commiffion by
ye whiche ye fhall wel perceyue yat I fpeake nothyng
vpon my own head, but euery thyng according to the
commaundement of the Lorde your god, whyche hath
fent me vnto you hys people. The example of this
proclamacion. Ef. lviii. *Clama*.[3] Make proclamation
openly, yat al men maye heare: *ne ceffes*.[3] Ceas not
for feare of them that may kyll the body, and can not
hurt the foule, *quafi tuba exalta uocem tuam*,[3] Lifte vp
thy voyce as a trumpet, geuinge men knowledge of the

[1] Rom. xi. 32. [2] Act. iv [3] Isa. lviii. 1.

commyng of the ennemyes in the tyme of war. So geue them knowlege of the fwerd of vengeance, which fhal folow immediatli after this warning *Et annuncia populo meo fcelera eorum.*[1] And fhew them their fau[l]tes yat in bering of my name, and profeffinge my religion wil be my people. *Et domui Iacob peccata fua,*[1] and vnto the houfe of Iacob their own fins: vnto all fortes of men euen thofe fyns which they them felues do vfe. Vnto the clergy, the finnes of ye clergy, vnto the laitye, the fynnes of the layte: and vnto euery degre, ye finnes yat be of that degre vfed. Shew ye clergi that thei fede them felues fat with many liuings, and let my flocke be fcatered and vnfed, becaufe ther is few preching paftors yat can and wil fede them.

Shew the clergy that they can neyther teach, nor requyre the king and laitye to prouide new liuings for prechers, vntill they do reftore forth of their own hands thofe which be prouided alredy: fhew fuch of the cleargy as be fatlings puft vp with pluralities, that they neyther haue fed, do fede, or can fede my flocke, yet haue fpoyled, do fpoyle and wyl fpoyle my lambes, ye kynges fubiectes, and theyr own brethren, fo long as thei vfe their pluralities. Shew the laity yat thei haue robbed me theyr lord and god of double honour due vnto my mynifters: for they haue taken awaye the fodder that was prepared for the laborynge oxe, and bene difobedyent vnto my law, pronounced by theim that fate in Moyfes cheire.

Shewe the nobilitie that they haue oppreffed the comminaltye, Kepyng theim vnder in feare and ignorance, by power and aucthoritye, which myght and fhould haue bene louyngly learned their obedience and duty to both God and the kyng by preachyng of the gofpel. Shew the nobility yat they haue extorted and famifhed the commynalty by the heigthening of fynes and rentes of fermes, and decaying of hofpitality and good houfe kepyng. Shew the comminaltye yat they be both traytoures and rebelles, murmuryng and

[1] Isa. *lviii.* 1.

grudgyng agaynſt myne ordinaunces: tel the comminalty yat the oxe draweth, the horſe beareth, ye tre bryngeth forth frutes and the earthe corne and graſſe to the profyte and comforte of man, as I haue ordained them: but they of the comminaltye in England bye and ſel, make bargaynes, and do al thynges to the greſe and hynderaunce of manne, contrary to my commaundemente. Tell the commynaltye that they take one anothers ferme ouer their heades, they thruſte one an other oute of their houſes, they take leaſes vnto theim ſelues, and lette theym dearer vnto other: they bye cornes and wares to make other paye more dere for it: they hurte and trouble, eate vp and deuoure one another. Tell all Englande hye and low, riche and poore that they euerye one prowlynge for them ſelues, be ſeruaunts vnto Mammon, ennemies vnto god, diſturbers of common wealth, and deſtroyers of them ſelues. And for all this lette theim knowe that I haue no pleaſure in ye death of a ſinner. *Sed magis vt conuertatur et uiuat*,[1] but rather I geue him reſpit and ſend him warning yat he may turne and liue, comfortably here vpon earth, and ioifully in heauen for euer. Therefore if any in Englande do tourne and amende, he ſhall ſaue hym ſelfe. But they which wyll not repent and amend ſhal not be ſaued by theyr fathers or frendes, which by repentaunce be as ſure them ſelues to be accepted vnto me as was Noe Danyel and Iob: but and if all or the mooſt parte of them in England, turne and amend them, ſay vnto England: *delectaberis ſuper domino*.[2] From henceforth you ſhalt haue delite and pleſure in ye lord, *et ſuſtollam te ſuper altitudines terræ*,[2] and I wil lift the higher in honour welth and power, then any other realme in or vpon the earth, *et cibabo te hereditate Iacobi patris tui*,[2] and ſo wyll I fede the with the inheritaunce of Iacob thy father. I will reſtore vnto ye whatſoeuer land or holds in Scotland or in Fraunce dyd at any tyme belonge vnto Iacob thy father, vnto the kings of this realme, *os enim domini locutum eſt*,[2] for the Lordes owne mouth

[1] Ezek *xxviii*. 11.   [2] Isa. *lviii*. 14.

hath fpoken it, which is a better affurance vnto this
commiffion, then though it were figned and feled wyth
ten thoufande mens handes.

Now al you yat entend to be faued by the mercies
of god in our fauioure Iefu Chrift, come when ye be
called from gredy couetoufnes wherwyth ye haue bene
blinded to wreake Gods wrath: receyue mercy and
grace which be now frely offred to make you from
henceforth holy minifters of Chrift, and faithfull difpofers of ye manifolde gyftes of Gods grace and goodnes: and now for fere of forgetfull negligence, when ye
depart hence, replenifh your minds with ye comfortable remembrance of your own greuous myferies, and
of gods great mercies, in fecrete meditation of the
lords praier, here tarying together in quyetnes a littell
for to receyue the Lordes bleffyng.

The god of peace that brought againe from death
our Lord Iefus the greate fhepeheard of the fhepe,
thorow the bloud of the euerlaftyng teftament, make
you perfit in all good workes, to do hys wyll, workyng
in you that which is plefant in his
fyght, through Iefus Chrift.
Amen.

God faue the Kynge.[1]

---

[1] In second edition, 1572.   God saue the Queene.

Imprynted at London by Ihon Day dwellyng ouer Alderfgate.

Cum priuilegio ad imprimendum folum Per feptennium.

In the reprint of 1572, the colophon is—

to be folde at the litle at the signe of the blacke Boye.

Muir & Paterson, Printers, Edinburgh.

1 OCTOBER 1870.

Please oblige, by showing this List to your friends.

Works in English Literature

PUBLISHED OR TO BE PUBLISHED BY

EDWARD ARBER,

Associate, King's College, London, F.R.G.S., &c.

AT

5 QUEEN SQUARE, BLOOMSBURY, LONDON, W.C.

Sold by all Booksellers in the United Kingdom, and by the following, abroad :—

Berlin: N. ASHER.	Montreal: DAWSON BROTHERS.
Bombay: THACKER, VINING & CO.	New York: SCRIBNER, WELFORD & CO.
Boston: LITTLE, BROWN & CO.	Philadelphia: C. J. PRICE.
Calcutta: THACKER, SPINK & CO.	San Francisco: A. L. BANCROFT & CO.
Melbourne: GEORGE ROBERTSON.	Toronto: ADAM, STEVENSON & CO.

*** Foreign booksellers selling these publications can have their names added to the above, in the next List, upon application.

CHRONOLOGICAL LIST.	2
FOR STUDENTS OF ENGLISH LITERATURE.	
TO STUDENTS.	3
Facsimile Texts.	4
English Reprints, Foolscap size.	5–12
Demy size.	13
Imperial size.	14
Annotated Reprints. (THE PASTON LETTERS.)	15
FOR GENERAL READERS.	
Leisure Readings in English Literature.	16
Choice Books.	16

These publications are all edited by Mr. Arber, unless otherwise stated.

Any single work may be obtained separately. In ordering quote the NUMBER, TITLE, and PRICE (the author's name is unnecessary).

All orders must be accompanied by a remittance; which, if under 10s., can be made in *Postage Stamps*; if above that sum, in P.O.O., made payable at HIGH HOLBORN Office, or Cheques crossed LONDON AND COUNTY BANK.

These publications are ALWAYS on sale; and may be obtained through your own Bookseller; or, *in any number*, post free *by return*, on remitting to Mr. ARBER, *the prices*, as stated in this List.

The usual allowance to Colleges and Schools.

All inquiries must be accompanied by a Stamp for reply.

Subscriptions, of not less than One Guinea, can be paid in advance of the appearance of the Publications ordered.

This List cancels all previous ones, as regards Works not yet published.

Richard I.
1196. 1486. *The Revelation to the Monk of Evesham.* . No. 18

Henry IV.—Henry VII.
1422-1509. *The Paston Letters.* . . . .

Henry VIII.
1516. 1556. Sir T. More. *Utopia.* 14
1527. W. Roy. *Rede me and be nott wrothe.*
1530 [Roy?] *A proper dyaloge betwene a Gentillman, etc.*
1545. R. Ascham. *Toxophilus.* . . . 7

Edward VI.
1549. Bp. H. Latimer. *The Ploughers.* . . 2
1549. Do. *Seven Sermons before Ed. VI.* . 13
1550. Rev. T. Lever. *Sermon in the Shrouds of St. Pauls.* 25
1550. Do. *Sermon before Ed. VI.* . . 25
1550. Do. *Sermon at Paul's Cross.* . . 25
1553. 1566. N. Udall. *Roister Doister.* . . . 17
1553. R. Eden. *Translation from S. Munster (1532).*

Philip and Mary.
1555. R. Eden. *Translations from Peter Martyr (1516).*
? Oviedo y Valdes (1521), A. Pigafetta (1532), etc.
1557. Tottel's *Miscellany, Songes and Sonettes, etc.* . 24

Elizabeth.
1562. 1563. B. Googe. *Eglogs, Epytaphes, etc.*
1570. R. Ascham. *The Scholemaster.* . . 23
1575. G. Gascoigne. *Notes of Instruction in Eng. verse.* 11
1576. G. Gascoigne. *The complaynt of Philomene.* . 11
1576. Do. *The Stele Glasse.* . . 11
1577. G. Whetstone. *A Remembrance of G. Gascoigne.* 11
1579. J. Lyly. *Euphues. The Anatomy of Wit.* . 9
1579. S. Gosson. *The Schoole of Abuse.* . . 3
1579. Do. *An Apologie for the School of Abuse.* 3
1580. J. Lyly. *Euphues and his England.* . . 9
1557-1580. T. Tusser. *Fine Hundred Points of Good Husbandrie.* 4
1582. 1595. Sir P. Sidney. *An Apologie for Poetrie.* . 21
1582. T. Watson. *The Ἑκατομπαθία.*
1583. Rev. P. Stubbes. *The Anatomie of Abuses.*
1583. Do. *2d Part of The Anatomie of Abuses.*
1586. James VI. *The Essayes of a Prentise in. . Poesie.* 10
1586. W. Webbe. *A Discourse of English Poetry.* . 26

1589. G. Puttenham. *The Arte of English Poesie.* No. 15
1590. Ubaldini.—Rytuer. *Conceryng the Spanishe fleete.* 21
1590. T. Watson. *Meliboeus.* . . . 21
1590. Do. *An Eclogue, &c.* . . . 21
1590. E. Webbe. *His Wonderful Travailes.* . . 5
1591. Sir W. Ralegh. *The Fight in the 'Revenge.'*
1592. 1593. T. Watson. *The Teares of Fancy or Love disdained.* 21
1593. *The Phœnix Nest.* Ed. by R. S.
1595. G. Markham. *The Tragedie of Sir R. Grenville.*
1597. F. Bacon. *Essayes.*

James I.
1604. [James I.] *A Counterblaste to Tobacco.* . 19
1612-12. Sir F. Bacon. *The Writings, &c. &c.* Harl. MS. 5106.
1612. *The Essaies of Sir F. Bacon, Knt.*
? 1653. Sir R. Naunton. *Fragmenta Regalia.* . . 20

Charles I.
1625. Francis Lord Verulam, *Essayes or Counsels.*
1628-33. Bp. J. Earle. *Microcosmographie.* . . 12
1625-45. J. Selden. *Table Talk.* . . . 6
1634-40. W. Habington. *Castara.* . . . 22
1637. Star Chamber. *Decree concerning Printing.*
1640. F. Quarles. *Enchyridion.*
1641. J. Milton. *The Reason of Church Government, etc.*
1642. J. Howell. *Instructions for Forreine Travell.* 16
1643. Lords and Commons. *Order regulating of Printing.* 1
1644. J. Milton. *On Education.*
1644. Do. *Areopagitica.*
1645. J. Howell. *Epistolæ Ho-Elianæ.* Book I.
1647. J. Howell. *Epistolæ Ho-Elianæ.* Book II.

Commonwealth.
1650. J. Howell. *Epistolæ Ho-Elianæ.* Book III.
1650. Do. *Instructions for travelling into Turkey.* 18
1655. Do. *Epistolæ Ho-Elianæ.* Book IV.

Charles II.
1671. 1672. G. Villiers, Duke of Buckingham, *The Rehearsal.* 10

William and Mary.
1694. E. Phillips. *Life of John Milton.*

Anne.
1712. J. Addison. *Criticism on Paradise Lost.* . 8

URELY to us, after the Sacred Scriptures, works of devotion and of religious instruction; the Literature of England comes next. However exquisite and subtle the charms of Greek and Grecian literature; however necessary and worthy of study the language and literature of Rome; the writings of our Forefathers come home to every Englishman. What a mighty Literature have we inherited! How little is it known, save to a few, who have devoted all their leisure to its exploration! Authors mighty in Prose and Verse! Writers full of aëry fancies and graceful similitudes! Men whose Prose marches with the tramp and strength of a Roman legion: men whose Song is sung by a Puck or an Ariel; or who sing in it of Patient Grissell, of Fair Geraldine, or of Una and her Red Cross Knight. Above all the English Bible, so clung unto by our ancestors—with its infinite early editions and their most heroic story.

What present nation has so ancient, so vast, so varied a body of writings as England? In which are contained not only the productions of our Arch-Poets, Chaucer, Spenser, Shakespeare, Milton, Dryden; but those of an almost uncountable number of authors, inferior indeed to these, but of high rank among ordinary minds.

Good books, besides affording enjoyment, provoke to like excellence. No man writeth unto himself. Each worthy writer is trained, assimilated, and influenced by those who have gone before: each returning a like benefit to posterity. To trace the continuous chain of influence, of cause and effect, link by link, forms a part of the History of English Literature. That History that we may soon hope to possess, for the first time adequately in our language, in Professor HENRY MORLEY's work *English Writers*: of which we have already received the earlier instalment, down to Dunbar. What is designed in the *Facsimile Texts*, the *English Reprints*, and the *Annotated Reprints* is to *represent* the later literature by giving, at as cheap a price as can be, Exact Texts sometimes of books already famous, sometimes of those quite forgotten: in some cases, of works that illustrate the Literary History; in other instances, of those that in a sense, constitute it.

The result is already, that these Reproductions are unique in English Bibliography for their accuracy and cheapness, as well as for the unlimited numbers offered constantly for sale: and *so far as they are yet published*, they constitute the best of all introductions to our old Authors, from the time of Caxton to that of Addison.   E. A.

P.S.—A word in furtherance of the *Early English Text*, the *Chaucer*, and the *Ballad* Societies. No one knows the extent of the unprinted Literature of England. These Societies are recovering for us book after book; and laying us all under great obligation to their able Editors, who labour gratuitously. For further information, apply to F. J. Furnivall, M.A., 3 St. George's Square, London, N.W.

Facsimile Texts.

In Varying Sizes, following the Originals.

F European publications there are not a few which the mere outward appearance, their countenance so to speak, possess an extreme interest. Either from the excessive rarity of the book itself, or the drollery or quaintness of its illustrations; either from the literary importance of the work or its significance in the history of our Country or in the progress of the World : there arises at the sight of it the keenest attention, one might almost say an inexpressible sympathy with the book itself. In all such cases: Sun-Portraits confer exquisite and perpetual enjoyment.

Hitherto Cost has debarred photolithographed books from general use; but I trust to offer from time to time, at *ordinary book-prices*, works of this supreme interest, though necessarily of an infinitely diverse character. In which effort, I trust to receive a thorough support from the large number of readers who have sustained the *English Reprints*. Both being like attempts to make forgotten books known; and known books, more perfectly and perpetually obtainable.

Early in November, will be published in Fcp. 4to., Half Calf, Illuminated sides, pp. xxxii.-64.

[WILLIAM TYNDALE, assisted by WILLIAM ROY.

The First *printed* English New Testament. Cologne—Worms. 1525. 4to.]

Photo-lithographed, by the permission of the Trustees of the British Museum, from the *unique* fragment in the Grenville Collection.

Briefly told, the story of this profoundly interesting work is as follows :—In 1524 TYNDALE went from London to Hamburg; where remaining for about a year, he journeyed on to Cologne; and there assisted by WILLIAM ROY, subsequently the author of the Satire on Wolsey, *Rede me and be nott wrothe* [see *p.* 11], he began this first edition in 4to; *with glosses* of the English New Testament. A virulent enemy of the Reformation, COCHLÆUS, at that time an exile in Cologne, learnt, through giving wine to the printer's men, that P. Quentel the printer had in hand a secret edition of three thousand copies of the English New Testament. In great alarm, he informed Herman Rinck, Senator of the city, who moved the Senate to stop the printing; but Cochlæus could neither obtain a sight of the Translators, nor a sheet of the impression.

Tyndale and Roy, fled with the printed sheets, up the Rhine to Worms; and there completing this edition, produced also another in Octavo, *without glosses*. Both editions were in England in Jan.-March, 1526: and of the six thousand copies of which they together were composed, there remain but this fragment of the First commenced edition; and of the Second edition, one complete copy in the Library of the Baptist College at Bristol, and an imperfect one in that of St. Paul's Cathedral, London.

The price of this *Facsimile Text*, will be only SIX SHILLINGS.

English Reprints.   5

THE great importance to the increasing study of English Literature, of constantly adding to, and constantly keeping on sale (a more difficult task than at first would appear) at the lowest practicable prices, these Exact Texts; has led to a full consideration of the past three years' progress, in an experiment which has been successful beyond anticipation. The following alterations have been found advisable, in order to place this designedly very cheap Series upon a permanent basis.

The changes to take effect from 1st October 1870.

Small Paper, in Foolscap Octavo.

1. The public choice has passed so generally from *Cut* to *Uncut* edges: that future issues will be in *Uncut* edges only. This will also apply to all reimpressions, as soon as the existing *Cut-edged* copies have been sold.

2. No Sixpenny Reprints will be issued in future. The trouble is out of all proportion to the price.

3. The *maximum* number of pages for Shilling works will be about One hundred and twenty-eight. Experience has proved that number to be the *very utmost* limit practicable for such closely packed works in the costly old spelling, &c.

∴ The result of these changes to the public will be simply, that some future Reprints will be increased in price, by an extra Sixpence. A trifling contribution to enable me to go on for years. Yet I very reluctantly decide on this augmentation: this series being my personal free offering to a more perfect knowledge of English Literature.

All existing issues will be maintained at the present prices.

Large Paper, in Foolscap Quarto.

Nos. 19 to 24 in Large Paper are now ready. A single Large Paper copy can be obtained.

Demy Quarto.

Works in this size will be issued bound in Cloth. When published, copies will however be obtainable in Sheets, for binding, by remitting the price *direct* to me.

There is a great cause for thankfulness in the progress already made. Works which some of our most experienced English scholars never hoped to see reprinted; have been put into *general* circulation. Much more may be accomplished, by a personal advocacy of this Series by *each* Purchaser; with a generous permission to print, from possessors of rare or unique English books; and with unwearying effort on my own part. Maintaining herein the ancient and worthy fame of England; may we lead very many to understand how much pure and unadulterated Delight is to be found in our Old English Authors.

English Reprints.

ORDINARY ISSUE IN OCTAVO.

Durable Cases, in Roxburghe style, to hold four or five Reprints. One Shilling each.

BOUND VOLUMES IN OCTAVO.

Two or three of such works, collected into occasional Volumes.

LARGE PAPER EDITION IN QUARTO.

The same texts, beautifully printed on thick toned paper, with ample margins suitable for purposes of study. Issued in Stiff covers, uncut edges. When bound to the purchaser's own taste; these Large Paper Copies form most handsome books.

ANY SINGLE WORK OR VOLUME MAY BE HAD SEPARATELY.

Quarto.	FOOLSCAP.	Octavo.
Large Paper Edit.		Stiff Covers. Uncut Edges.	Green Cloth. Red Edges.
	1. JOHN MILTON.	
	(1) A decree of the Starre-Chamber, concerning Printing, made the eleuenth day of July last past. London, 1637.	
	(2) An Order of the Lords and Commons assembled in Parliament for the regulating of Printing, &c. London, 14 June, 1643.	
1/6	(3) *AREOPAGITICA*: A speech of Mr. John Milton for the liberty of Vnlicenc'd Printing, to the Parliament of England. London. [24 November]. 1644. **Sixpence.**	Vol. I.
	2. HUGH LATIMER, *Ex-Bishop of Worcester.*	Milton,
1/6	*SERMON ON THE PLOUGHERS.* A notable Sermon of ye reuerende father Master Hughe Latimer, whiche he preached in ye Shroudes at paules churche in London, on the xviii daye of Januarye. ☾ The yere of our Loorde MDXLviii. **Sixpence.**	Latimer, Gosson.
	3. STEPHEN GOSSON, *Stud. Oxon.*	
	(1) *THE SCHOOLE OF ABUSE.* Conteining a pleasaunt invective against Poets, Pipers, Plaiers, Jesters, and such like Caterpillers of a Commonwealth; Setting up the Flagge of Defiance to their mischievous exercise, and ouerthrowing their Bulwarkes, by Prophane Writers, Naturall reason, and common experience. A discourse as pleasaunt for gentlemen that fauour learning, as profitable for all that wyll follow vertue. London. [August?] 1579.	2/
1/6	(2) *AN APOLOGIE OF THE SCHOOLE OF ABUSE*, against Poets, Pipers, and their Excusers. London. [December?] 1579. **Sixpence.**	
	4. SIR PHILIP SYDNEY.	
1/6	*AN APOLOGIE FOR POETRIE.* Written by the right noble, vertuous and learned Sir Philip Sidney, Knight. London. 1595. **Sixpence.**	

ENGLISH REPRINTS—FOOLSCAP.

Quarto.   Octavo.
Large Paper Edit.   TITLES, PRICES, etc., etc.   Stiff Covers. | Green Cloth, Uncut Edges. | Red Edges.

5. EDWARD WEBBE, *Chief Master Gunner.*

   The rare and most vvonderful thinges which Edward Webbe an Englishman borne, hath seene and passed in his troublesome trauailes, in the Citties of Ierusalem, Damasko, Bethelem, and Galely: and in the Landes of Iewrie, Egipt, Grecia, Russia, and in the land of Prester Iohn. Wherein is set foorth his extreame slauerie sustained many yeres togither, in the Gallies and wars of the great Turk against the Landes of Persia, Tartaria, Spaine, and Portugall, with the manner of his releasement, and comming into London in May last. London. 1590.
                                                          Sixpence.

1/6 — Vol. II. — Sidney, Webbe, Selden. 2/6

6. JOHN SELDEN.

   TABLE TALK: being the Discourses of John Selden Esq.; or his Sence of various Matters of Weight and High Consequence relating especially to Religion and State. London. 1689.   <u>One Shilling.</u>

2/6

7. ROGER ASCHAM.

   TOXOPHILUS. The schole of shooting conteyned in tvvo bookes. To all Gentlemen and yomen of Englande, pleasaunte for theyr pastime to rede, and profitable for theyr use to folow, both in warre and peace. London. 1545.   <u>One Shilling.</u>

2/6 — Vol. III. — Ascham, Addison. 2/6

8. JOSEPH ADDISON.

   CRITICISMS OF MILTON'S PARADISE LOST. From *The Spectator:* being its Saturday issues between 31 December, 1711, and 3 May, 1712. <u>One Shilling.</u>

2/6

9. JOHN LYLY, M.A.

   (1) ¶ *EUPHUES. THE ANATOMY OF WIT.* Verie pleasaunt for all Gentlemen to read, and most necessarie to remember. Wherein are contained the delightes that Wit followeth in his youth by the pleasantnesse of loue, and the happinesse he reapeth in age, by the perfectnesse of Wisedome. London. 1579.

   (2) ¶ *EUPHUES AND HIS ENGLAND.* Containing his voyage and aduentures, myxed with sundrie pretie discourses of honest Loue, the Description of the Countrey, the Court, and the manners of that Isle. Delightful to be read, and nothing hurtful to be regarded: wher-in there is small offence by lightnesse giuen to the wise, and lesse occasion of loosenes proferred to the wanton. London, 1580. Collated with early subsequent editions.   <u>Four Shillings.</u>

9/ — Vol. IV. — Lyly. 5/

8   ENGLISH REPRINTS—FOOLSCAP.

Quarto.		Octavo.
Large Paper Edit.	TITLES, PRICES, etc., etc. Stiff Covers. Uncut Edges.	Green Cloth. Red Edges.

10. GEORGE VILLIERS, *Duke of Buckingham.*
    THE REHEARSAL. As it was acted at the Theatre Royal London, 1672. With Illustrations from previous

2/6 plays, &c.   **One Shilling.**

11. GEORGE GASCOIGNE, *Esquire.*
    (1) A remembravnce of the wel imployed life, and godly end of George Gaskoigne, Esquire, who deceassed at Stalmford in Lincoln shire, the 7 of October 1577. The reporte of GEOR WHETSTONS, Gent an eye witness of his Godly and Charitable End in this world. Lond. 1577.
    (2) Certayne notes of Instruction concerning the making of verse or rime in English, vvritten at the request of Master *Edouardi Donati.* 1575.
    (3) *THE STEELE GLAS.* A Satyre compiled by George Gasscoigne Esquire [Written between Apr. 1575 & Apr. 1576]. Together with
    (4) *THE COMPLAYNT OF PHYLOMENE.* An Elegie compyled by George Gasscoigne Esquire [between

2/6 April 1562 and 3rd April 1575.] London. 1576.
                                                               One Shilling.

Vol. V.

Villiers,

Gascoigne.

Earle.

3/6

12. JOHN EARLE, M.A.: *afterwards in succession Bishop of Worcester, and of Salisbury.*
    MICRO-COSMOGRAPHIE, or a Peece of the World discovered, in Essays and Characters. London. 1628. With the additions in subsequent editions during the

2 6 Author's life time.   **One Shilling.**

13. HUGH LATIMER, *Ex-Bishop of Worcester.*
    SEVEN SERMONS BEFORE EDWARD VI.
    (1) ¶ The fyrste sermon of Mayster Hugh Latimer, whiche he preached before the Kynges Maiest. wythin his graces palayce at Westmynster. M.D.XLIX. the viii of Marche. (,‘,)
    (2) The seconde [to seventh] Sermon of Master Hughe Latimer, whych he preached before the Kynges maiestie, withyn hys graces Palayce at Westminster ye. xv. day of

4/ March. M.cccc.xlix.   **Eighteen Pence.**

Vol. VI.

Latimer.

More.

3/

14. SIR THOMAS MORE.
    UTOPIA. A frutefull pleasaunt, and wittie worke, of the best state of a publique weale, and of the new yle, called Utopia: written in Latine, by the right worthie and famous Sir Thomas More knyght, and translated into Englishe by RAPHE ROBYNSON, sometime fellowe of Corpus Christi College in Oxford, and nowe by him at this seconde edition newlie perused and corrected, and also with divers notes in the margent augmented. London.

2/6 [1556].   **One Shilling.**

ENGLISH REPRINTS—FOOLSCAP. 9

Quarto. Large Paper Edit.	TITLES, PRICES, etc., etc.	Octavo.
		Stiff Covers. Uncut Edges. / Green Cloth, Red Edges.
5/	**15. GEORGE PUTTENHAM.** *THE ARTE OF ENGLISH POESIE.* Contriued into three Bookes: The first of Poets and Poesie, the second of Proportion, the third of Ornament. London. 1589. <u>Two Shillings.</u>	Vol. VII. Puttenham. 2/6
1/6	**16. JAMES HOWELL,** *Historiographer Royal to Charles II.* *INSTRUCTIONS FOR FORREINE TRAVELL.* Shewing by what *cours*, and in what *compasse of time*, one may take an exact Survey of the Kingdomes and States of Christendome, and arriue to the practicall knowledge of the Languages, to good purpose. London. 1642. Collated with the edition of 1656; and in its 'new Appendix for Travelling into *Turkey* and the *Levant* parts' added. <u>Sixpence.</u>	Vol. VIII.
1/6	**17. The earliest known English comedy. NICHOLAS UDALL,** *Master of Eton.* *ROISTER DOISTER*, [from the unique copy at Eton College]. 1566. <u>Sixpence.</u>	Howell. Udall.
2/6	**18.** *THE REVELATION TO THE MONK OF EVESHAM.* Here begynnyth a marvelous revelacion that was schewyd of almighty god by sent Nycholas to a monke of Euyshamme yn the days of Kynge Richard the fyrst. And the yere of our lord. M.C.Lxxxxvi. [From the unique copy, printed about 1482, in the British Museum]. <u>One Shilling.</u>	Monk of Evesham James VI. 3/6
2/6	**19. JAMES VI.** *of Scotland,* **I.** *of England.* (1) *THE ESSAYES OF A PRENTISE, IN THE DIVINE ART OF POESIE.* Edinburgh 1585. (2) *A COUNTER BLASTE TO TOBACCO.* London. 1604. <u>One Shilling.</u>	
1/6	**20. SIR ROBERT NAUNTON,** *Master of the Court of Wards.* *FRAGMENTA REGALIA:* or, Observations on the late Queen Elizabeth, her Times, and Favourites. [Third Edition. London] 1653. <u>Sixpence.</u>	Vol. IX. Naunton. Watson. 2/6
	21. THOMAS WATSON, *Student at law.* (1) *THE* Εκατομπαθια or Passionate Centurie of Loue. Divided into two parts: whereof, the first expresseth the Authors sufferance in Loue: the latter, his long farewell to Loue and all his tyrannie. Composed by *Thomas Watson* Gentleman; and published at the request of certaine Gentlemen his very frendes. London [1582.]	

Quarto. Large Paper Edit.	TITLES, PRICES, etc., etc.	Octavo. Stiff Covers. Uncut Edges.	Green Cloth, Red Edges.
4/	(2) *MELIBŒUS* T. Watsoni, Ecloga in obitum F. Walsinghami, &c. Londini, 1590. (3) *AN EGLOGUE*, &c., Written first in latine [the above MELIBŒUS] by *Thomas Watson* Gentleman and now by himselfe translated into English. London 1590. (4) *THE TEARS OF FANCY*, or Loue disdained. [From the unique copy, wanting Sonnets ix.-xvi., in the possession of S. Christie-Miller, Esq.] London, 1593. Eighteen Pence.		
2/6	**22. WILLIAM HABINGTON.** *CASTARA.* The third Edition. Corrected and augmented. London. 1640. With the variations of the two previous editions. One Shilling.		Vol. X. ——— Habington, Ascham. 2/6
2/6	**23. ROGER ASCHAM.** *THE SCHOLEMASTER*, Or plaine and perfite way of teachyng children, to vnderstand, write, and speake, the Latin tong, but specially purposed for the priuate brynging vp of youth in Ientlemen and Noble mens houses, commodious also for all such, as haue forgot the Latin tongue, and would, by themselues, without a Scholemaster, in short tyme, and with small paines, recouer a sufficient habilitie, to vnderstand, write, and speake Latin. London. 1570. One Shilling.		
6/6	**24. Tottel's Miscellany.** *SONGES AND SONETTES*, written by the ryght honorable Lorde HENRY HAWARD, late Erle of Surrey, and other. [London, 5 June] 1557. Half-a-crown.		Vol. XI. ——— Tottel. 3/
4/	**25. REV. THOMAS LEVER, M.A. :** *afterwards Master of St John's College, Cambridge.* *SERMONS.* (1) A fruitfull Sermon made in Paules churche at London in the Shroudes, the second of Februari. 1550. (2) A Sermon preached the thyrd [or fourth] Sunday in Lent before the Kynges Maiestie, and his honourable counsell. 1550. (3) A Sermon preached at Pauls Crosse, the xiiii. day of December 1550. Eighteen Pence.		Vol. XII. ——— Lever, Webbe. 3/
2/6	**26. WILLIAM WEBBE,** *Graduate.* *A DISCOURSE OF ENGLISH POETRIE.* Together, with the Authors iudgment, touching the reformation of our English Verse. London. 1586. One Shilling.		

∴ *The following works are designed for publication in time to come. Their prices cannot be fixed with precision, but are approximately given.* Ferrex and Porrex *has been postponed; and*

Newes from the North by F. T. [FRANCIS THYNNE], *with* RICHARD BARNFIELD'S Poems *have not been inserted; some of the Texts not being accessible, at the present time.* J. HOWELL'S Epistolæ Ho-Elianæ *will be put to press as soon as No.* 27 BACON'S Essayes, &c., *is finished.*

Large Paper Edit.		Stiff Covers. Uncut Edges.	Green Cloth, Red Edges.
	27. FRANCIS BACON. A harmony of the *ESSAYES*, &c. The four principle texts appearing in parallel columns. ; (1) Essayes. Religious Meditations. Places of perswasion and disswasion. London 1597. (10 Essays.) Of the Coulers of good and euill a fragment. 1597. (2) The writings of Sir Francis Bacon Knt: the Kinges Sollicitor Generall: in Moralitie, Policie, and Historie. *Harleian MS.* 5106. Transcribed bet. 1607-12. (34 Essays.) (3) THE ESSAIES of Sir FRANCIS BACON Knight, the Kings Solliciter Generall. London 1612. (38 Essays.) (4) The Essayes or Counsels, Ciuill and Morall, of FRANCIS LO. VERULAM Viscount ST. ALBANS. *Newly Written.* 1626. (58 Essays.)		Vol. XIII. Bacon. 3/6
7/6		Three Shillings.	
	28. WILLIAM ROY, *Franciscan Friar.* (1) *REDE ME AND BE NOTT WROTHE.* [Strasburg. 1527. This is his famous Satire on Wolsey.] (2) *A PROPER DYALOGE BETWEEN A GENTLEMAN AND A HUSBANDMAN,* &c. [Attributed to Roy] Marburg. 1530. Eighteen Pence.		Vol. XIV. Roy.
2/6			
	29. SIR W. RALEIGH—G. MARKHAM. *THE LAST FIGHT OF THE REVENGE AT SEA.* (1) A report of the Truth of the fight about the Isles of Acores, this last Sommer. Betvvixt the Reuenge, one of her Maiesties Shippes, and an Armada of the King of Spaine. By Sir Walter Raleigh. London. 1591. (2) The most Honorable Tragedie of Sir Richarde Grinuille, Knight (.'.). *Bramo assai, poco spero, nulla chieggio.* [By GERVASE MARKHAM] London. 1595. [Two copies only are known, Mr. Grenville's cost £40.] One Shilling.		Fight in the Revenge. Googe. 4/
2/6			
	30. BARNABE GOOGE. *EGLOGS, EPYTAPHES AND SONETTES* newly written by Barnabe Googe. London 1563. 15 March. One Shilling.		
2/6			
	31. REV. PHILLIP STUBBES. (1) *THE ANATOMIE OF ABUSES:* conteyning a discoverie or briefe Summarie of Such Notable Vices and Imperfections, as now raigne in many Christian		

ENGLISH REPRINTS—FOOLSCAP.

Quarto. Large Paper Edit.	TITLES, PRICES, etc., etc.	Stiff Covers. Uncut Edges.	Octavo. Green Cloth, Red Edges.
6/6	Countreyes of the World: but especialie in a very famous ILANDE called AILGNA [i.e. Anglia]: Together with most fearefull Examples of Gods Iudgementes, executed vpon the wicked for the same, aswell in AILGNA of late, as in other places, elsewhere. . . London. 1 Maij. 1583. (2) The Second part of *THE ANATOMIE OF ABUSES.* . . . London. 1583. **Half-a-crown.**		Vol. Stubbes. 3/
	32. THOMAS TUSSER.		
4/	*FIVE HUNDRED POINTES OF GOOD HUS-BANDRIE,* as well for the Champion, or open Countrie, as also for the woodland, or Seuerall, mixed in euery Month with *HUSWIFERIE,* . . . with diuers other lessons, as a diet for the former, of the properties of windes, plantes, hops, herbes, bees and approued remedies for sheepe and cattle, with many other matters both profitable and not vnpleasant for the Reader . . . . London. 1580. **Eighteen Pence.**		Vol. Tusser.
	33. JOHN MILTON.		Milton.
2/6	(1) The Life of Mr John Milton [by his nephew EDWARD PHILLIPS]. From '*Letters of State written by Mr. John Milton,* bet. 1649-59.' London. 1694. (2) *THE REASON OF CHURCH GOVERNE-MENT* urg'd against Prelacy. By Mr. *John Milton.* In two Books. [London] 1641. (3) Milton's Letter *OF EDUCATION.* To Master *Samuel Hartlib.* [London. 5 June 1644.] **One Shilling.**		3/
	34. FRANCIS QUARLES.		
2/6	*ENCHYRIDION,* containing Institutions { Divine { Contemplative. / Practicall. / Ethycall. } Morall { Oeconomicall. / Politicall. } London. 1640-1. **One Shilling.**		Vol. Quarles.
	35. The Sixth English Poetical Miscellany.		The Phœnix Nest.
2/6	*THE PHOENIX NEST.* Built vp with the most rare and refined workes of Noble men, woorthy Knights, gallant Gentlemen, Masters of Arts, and braue Schoolers. Full of varietie, excellent inuention, and singular delight. *Never before this time published.* Set forth by R. S. of the Inner Temple Gentleman. London 1593. **One Shilling.**		2/6
	36. SIR THOMAS ELYOT.		Vol. Elyot.
6/6	*THE GOVERNOR.* The boke named the Gouernor, deuised by ye Thomas Elyot Knight. Londini M.D.xxxi. Collated with subsequent editions. **Half-a-crown.**		3/

Demy Quarto.

Will be ready, about March 1871, *in one Volume,* 12s. 6d.

801. RICHARD EDEN.

I. A treatyse OF THE NEWE INDIA, WITH OTHER NEW FOUNDE LANDES AND ISLANDS, ASWELL EASTWARDE AS WESTWARDE, as they are knowen and found in these oure dayes, after the descripcion of SEBASTIAN MUNSTER, in his boke of vniuersall Cosmographie, &c. [London, 1553.]

II. The First English Collection of Voyages, Traffics, and Discoveries.— THE DECADES OF THE NEW WORLD OR WEST INDIA, &c. &c. [by Peter Martyr of Angleria.] [Translated, compiled, &c. by Richard Eden.]   Londini, Anno 1555.

1. The [Dedicatory] Epistle [to King Philip and Queen Mary.]
2. Richard Eden to the Reader.
3. The [1st, 2nd, and 3d only of the 8] Decades of the newe worlde or west India, Conteynyng the nauigations and conquestes of the Spanyardes, with the particular description of the moste ryche and large lands and Ilandes lately founde in the west Ocean perteynyng to the inheritance of the kinges of Spayne. In the which the diligent reader may not only consyder what commoditie may hereby chaunce to the hole christian world in tyme to come, but also learne many secreates touchynge the lande, the sea, and the starres, very necessarie to be knowen to al such as shal attempte any nauigations, or otherwise haue delite to beholde the strange and woonderful woorkes of god and nature. Wrytten in the Latine tounge by PETER MARTYR of Angleria, and translated into Englysshe by RYCHARDE EDEN.
4. The Bull of Pope Alexander VI. in 1493, granting to the Spaniards 'the Regions and Ilandes founde in the Weste Ocean' by them.
5. *The Historic of the West Indies* by GONÇALO FERNANDEZ OVIEDO Y VALDES.
6. Of other notable things gathered out of dyuers autors.
7. Of Moscouie and Cathay.
8. Other notable thynges as touchynge the Indies [chiefly out of the books of FRANCISCO LOPEZ DE GOMARA, 'and partly also out of the caade made by SEBASTIAN CABOT.']
9. The Booke of Metals.
10. The description of the two viages made owt of England into Guinea in Affricke [1553, 1554].
11. The maner of fyndynge the Longitude of regions.

INDEX.

.·. An abridged analysis of this voluminous work was issued in the previous catalogue (1 Dec. 1869); which will be found bound up with 'English Reprints' issued during this year, 1870.

Imperial Folio.

1001. PETRUCCIO UBALDINI—AUGUSTINE RYTHER.

A Discourse concerning the Spanishe fleete inuadinge Englande in the yeare 1588 and ouerthrowne by her Maiesties Nauie vnder the conduction of the Right-honorable the Lorde Charles Howarde highe Admirall of Englande: written in Italian by PETRUCCIO VBALDINI citizen of Florence, and translated for A. RYTHER: vnto the which discourse are annexed certain tables expressinge the generall exploites, and conflictes had with the said fleete.

These bookes with the tables belonginge to them are to be solde at the shoppe of A. RYTHER, being a little from Leaden hall next to the Signe of the Tower. [1590.]

The twelve Tables express the following subjects:—

FRONTISPIECE.

I. THE SPANISH ARMADA COMING INTO THE CHANNEL, OPPOSITE THE LIZARD; AS IT WAS FIRST DISCOVERED.

II. THE SPANISH ARMADA AGAINST FOWEY, DRAWN UP IN THE FORM OF A HALF MOON; THE ENGLISH FLEET PURSUING.

III. THE FIRST ENGAGEMENT BETWEEN THE TWO FLEETS. AFTER WHICH THE ENGLISH GIVE CHASE TO THE SPANIARDS, WHO DRAW THEIR SHIPS INTO A BALL.

IV. DE VALDEZ'S GALLEON SPRINGS HER FOREMAST, AND IS TAKEN BY SIR FRANCIS DRAKE. THE LORD ADMIRAL WITH THE 'BEAR' AND THE 'MARY ROSE,' PURSUE THE ENEMY, WHO SAIL IN THE FORM OF A HALF MOON.

V. THE ADMIRAL'S SHIP OF THE GUIPUSCOAN SQUADRON HAVING CAUGHT FIRE, IS TAKEN BY THE ENGLISH. THE ARMADA CONTINUES ITS COURSE, IN A HALF MOON; UNTIL OFF THE ISLE OF PORTLAND, WHERE ENSUES THE SECOND ENGAGEMENT.

VI. SOME ENGLISH SHIPS ATTACK THE SPANIARDS TO THE WESTWARD. THE ARMADA AGAIN DRAWING INTO A BALL, KEEPS ON ITS COURSE FOLLOWED BY THE ENGLISH.

VII. THE THIRD AND THE SHARPEST FIGHT BETWEEN THE TWO FLEETS: OFF THE ISLE OF WIGHT.

VIII. THE ARMADA SAILING UP CHANNEL TOWARDS CALAIS; THE ENGLISH FLEET FOLLOWING CLOSE.

IX. THE SPANIARDS AT ANCHOR OFF CALAIS. THE FIRESHIPS APPROACHING. THE ENGLISH PREPARING TO PURSUE.

X. THE FINAL BATTLE. THE ARMADA FLYING TO THE NORTHWARD. THE CHIEF GALLEASS STRANDED NEAR CALAIS.

LARGE MAP SHOWING THE TRACK OF THE ARMADA ROUND THE BRITISH ISLES.

These plates, which are a most valuable and early representation of the Spanish Invasion, are being re-engraved in *facsimile*, and will be issued in the Spring of 1871, at the lowest feasible price: probably HALF-A-GUINEA.

∴ *Other works may follow.*

BY VARIOUS EDITORS: UNDER MR. ARBER'S GENERAL SUPERVISION.

Some Texts require the amplest elucidation and illustration by Masters in special departments of knowledge. To recover and perpetuate such Works is to render the greatest service to Learning. With the aid of Scholars in special subjects, I hope to endow our readers with some knowledge of the Past, that is now quite out of their reach. While the Editors will be responsible both for Text and Illustrations; the works will be produced under my general oversight: so that the Annotated Reprints, though of much slower growth, will more than equal in value the English Reprints. E. A.

In the Spring of 1871 : in Fcp. 8vo the First Volume (to be completed in Four) of

The Paston Letters. 1422-1509.

Edited by JAMES GAIRDNER, Esq., of the Public Record Office.

EVERY one knows what a blank is the history of England during the Wars of the two Roses. Amid the civil commotions, literature almost died out. The principal poetry of the period is that of Lydgate, the Monk of Bury. The prose is still more scanty. The monastic Chronicles are far less numerous than at earlier periods: and by the end of the Fifteenth Century they seem to have entirely ceased. Thus it has come to pass that less is known of this age than of any other in our history. In this general dearth of information recent historians like Lingard, Turner, Pauli, and Knight, who have treated of the reigns of Henry VI., Edward IV., &c., have found in *The Paston Letters* not only unrivalled illustration of the Social Life of England, but also most important information, at first hand, as to the Political Events of that time. So that the printed Correspondence is cited page after page in their several histories of this period.

The Paston Letters have not however been half published. No literary use was made of them while accumulating in the family muniment room. William, 2nd Earl of Yarmouth, the last member of the family, having encumbered his inheritance, parted with all his property. The family letters came about 1728 into the hands of the distinguished antiquary, Peter le Neve; afterwards, by his marriage to Le Neve's widow, to his brother antiquary Martin of Palgrave; on his death again, to a Mr. Worth, from whom they were acquired by Mr. afterwards Sir John Fenn.

In 1787, Fenn published a small selection of the Letters in two volumes 4to; of which the first edition having been sold off in a week, a second appeared in the course of the year. He then prepared a further selection, of which two volumes appeared in 1789; the fifth volume being published after his death, in 1823.

Strangely enough, the Original Letters disappeared soon after their publication: and only those of the Fifth volume have, as yet, been recovered. There is no reasonable doubt that they still exist and will some day be found. There is no necessity, however, to postpone a new edition indefinitely, until they are again brought to light: for a comparison of the Fifth volume with its originals establishes Sir John Fenn's general faithfulness as to the Text; and therefore our present possession, in his Edition, of the contents of the missing Manuscripts.

Three hundred and eighty-seven letters in all were published by Fenn: about Four hundred additional letters or documents, belonging to the same collection and which have never been published at all, will be included in the present edition.

Not only will the Text be doubled in quantity; but in its elucidation, it will have the benefit of Mr. Gairdner's concentrated study of this Correspondence for years past. Half his difficulty will be in the unravelling of the chronology of the Letters, partly from internal evidence, partly from the Public Records, and other sources. Fenn's chronology—for no fault of his—is excessively misleading. This was inevitable, from the difficulties of a first attempt, the state of historic criticism in his day, and the limited means then available for consulting the public records, &c. It is hoped, however, by restoring each Letter to its certain or approximate date, vastly to increase the interest of this Correspondence. In addition textual difficulties will be removed, and valuable biographical information afforded.

The Letters of the reign of Henry VI. will form Vol. I. (estimated at about 600 *pp.*): those of Edward IV., Vols. II. and III. (together about 800 *pp.*): and those of Richard III. and Henry VII., Vol. IV. (about 300 *pp.*). The price will be *about* one shilling for every 100 *pp.*; and the work, it is expected, will be completed in Two years.

THE undermentioned modernized texts are in preparation. Great care will be bestowed in their transformation into the spelling and punctuation of the present day: but the Originals will be adhered to as closely as possible.

Leisure Readings in English Literature.

The object of the volumes that will appear under this general title, will be to afford Restful Reading; and, at the same time, by exhibiting the wealth of thought and the wit in expression of our Old Authors; to predispose to a further study of our Literature: in which study these Readings will serve as First Books.

They will contain many excellent Poems and Passages that are generally but very little known.

Choice Books.

THE DISASTROUS ENGLISH VOYAGE TO THE WEST INDIES IN 1568.

Recounted in the Narratives of Sir JOHN HAWKINS: and of DAVID INGRAM, MILES PHILLIPS, and JOB HORTOP, survivors, who escaped through the American Indian tribes; or out of the clutches of the Inquisition; or from the galleys of the King of Spain: and so at length came home to England.

∴ *Other works to follow.*

These works will be issued, beautifully printed and elegantly bound, in Crown 8vo.
The above is a specimen of the type, but not of the size of page.

---

5 QUEEN SQUARE, BLOOMSBURY, LONDON, W.C.

www.ingramcontent.com/pod-product-compliance
Lightning Source LLC
Chambersburg PA
CBHW030258170426
43202CB00009B/796